MW01121988

NEW ESSAYS ON CANADIAN THEATRE
VOLUME NINE

LINDA GRIFFITHS

NEW ESSAYS ON CANADIAN THEATRE
VOLUME NINE

LINDA GRIFFITHS
EDITED BY JACQUELINE PETROPOULOS

**Humber & University of
Guelph-Humber Library**
205 Humber College Blvd.
Toronto, ON M9W 5L7

PLAYWRIGHTS CANADA PRESS
TORONTO

Linda Griffiths © Copyright 2018 by Jacqueline Petropoulos
All essays herein are copyright © 2018 by their respective authors

First edition: November 2018
Printed and bound in Canada by Marquis Book Printing, Montréal

Playwrights Canada Press
202-269 Richmond Street West, Toronto, ON M5V 1X1
416.703.0013 :: info@playwrightscanada.com :: www.playwrightscanada.com

Cover photo of Linda Griffiths provided courtesy of Trudie Lee
Cover design by Leon Aureus

No part of this book may be reproduced, downloaded, or used in any form or by any means
without the prior written permission of the publisher, except for excerpts in a review or
by a licence from Access Copyright, www.accesscopyright.ca.

LIBRARY AND ARCHIVES CANADA CATALOGUING IN PUBLICATION
    Linda Griffiths / edited by Jacqueline Petropoulos. -- First edition.

(New essays on Canadian theatre; volume nine)
ISBN 978-1-77091-963-1 (softcover)

    1. Griffiths, Linda, 1953- --Criticism and interpretation.
I. Petropoulos, Jacqueline, 1973-, editor II. Series: New essays on
Canadian theatre ; v. 9

PS8563.R536Z73 2018   C812'.54   C2018-904733-X

Playwrights Canada Press acknowledges that we operate on land, which, for thousands
of years, has been the traditional territories of the Mississaugas of the New Credit, the
Huron-Wendat, the Anishinaabe, the Métis, and the Haudenosaunee peoples. Today, this
meeting place is home to many Indigenous peoples from across Turtle Island and we are
grateful to have the opportunity to work and play here.

We acknowledge the financial support of the Canada Council for the Arts—which last year
invested $153 million to bring the arts to Canadians throughout the country—the Ontario
Arts Council (OAC), the Ontario Media Development Corporation, and the Government
of Canada for our publishing activities.

CONTENTS

GENERAL EDITOR'S PREFACE
ROBERTA BARKER

When Ric Knowles founded New Essays in Canadian Theatre in 2011, he set out to complement his previous book series for Playwrights Canada Press, Critical Perspectives on Canadian Theatre in English (CPCTE). Each volume of the CPCTE series offered a critical history of a key topic in Canadian theatre studies; most of the essays featured in these volumes were reprints of important articles in the field, though they were supplemented by newly commissioned works that brought novel perspectives to the questions at hand. In NECT, Knowles chose to foreground new work, underexplored subjects, and fresh viewpoints. As he wrote in his General Editor's Preface for *Performing Indigeneity* (2016), these volumes

> are designed to fill what I perceive to be gaps in the critical record, often . . . taking new approaches, often . . . from minoritized and under-represented perspectives, and in almost every case introducing topics that have not received book-length coverage . . . [T]hey are designed at once to follow, lead, and instantiate new and emerging developments in the field. (v)

Responding to major questions of the present as well as to silences in the past, these books strive to shape the future of the field by opening exciting new avenues of exploration for artists, students, and scholars of Canadian theatre.

The six volumes published under Knowles's editorship richly fulfill this mandate, covering in the process a wide range of topics and approaches. Some, like *Asian Canadian Theatre* (edited by Nina Lee Aquino and Knowles) and *Latina/o Canadian Theatre and Performance* (edited by Natalie Alvarez), illuminate the vibrant and important work of key communities within the Canadian theatrical ecosystem. Others, like *New Canadian Realisms* (which I co-edited with Kim Solga) and *Theatres of Affect* (edited by Erin Hurley), strive to reconsider established genres and forms of theatre through new theoretical lenses. The 2015 volume, *Daniel MacIvor* (edited by Richie Wilcox), brings long overdue scholarly attention to the work of one of Canada's most beloved and innovative theatre artists. Finally, 2016's volume makes a particularly mighty contribution: *Performing Indigeneity*, edited by Yvette Nolan (Algonquin) and Knowles, is the first collection of essays on performance in Turtle Island to offer an all-Indigenous list of contributors. Many of these volumes, or the articles they feature, have been garlanded with scholarly prizes and awards: a fitting tribute to their impact on the field.

When I took over from Knowles as General Editor of NECT in 2017, I was both honoured and daunted by the task. Above all, I was inspired by the work of Knowles, his collaborators, and the many other brilliant scholars and artists who continue to transform our understanding of the field of Canadian theatre and performance. In the 2017 volume of NECT, *Canadian Performance Histories and Historiographies* (edited by Heather Davis-Fisch), a number of these writers set out to rethink the subject we have been used to calling "Canadian theatre history." The first 2018 volume, *Q2Q: Queer Canadian Theatre and Performance* (edited by Peter Dickinson, C.E. Gatchalian, Kathleen Oliver, and Dalbir Singh), brings together the voices of many of this country's leading makers and scholars of queer theatre and performance to explore, celebrate, debate, and at times redefine the ways in which LGBT2Q+ identities and perspectives have shaped theatre and performance on this land mass. Both of these volumes model Knowles's vision of the series as one that "takes new approaches" while foregrounding "minoritized and under-represented perspectives."

The present volume, edited by Jacqueline Petropoulos, is a unique collection for more reasons than one. It marks the first time Playwrights Canada Press has published two volumes in the NECT series within the span of one year; it is also the first ever edited collection to focus solely upon the work of the late, great Canadian theatre artist, Linda Griffiths. These two "firsts" are closely linked to one another. After Griffiths's untimely death in 2014, many members of the Canadian theatre community remembered her disappointment at the comparative lack of scholarly attention to her work. Perhaps scholars—like so many others in this land—took it too much for granted that the unquenchably vibrant Griffiths would always be there, always creating new work, always provoking new discussions. Once—shockingly—she was gone, they wished to honour her remarkable contribution to Canadian theatre while the image of her immense vitality was still vivid in the minds of her many colleagues, audience members, readers, and friends.

Though under-represented in scholarly publications to date, Griffiths's career richly deserves book-length coverage. Her early work with Paul Thompson (who pays tribute to her in this volume) and their many gifted collaborators gave birth to some indelible moments in Canadian theatre history. With *Maggie and Pierre* (1980), Griffiths seemed to crystallize a whole, heady era within a few movements on stage. With *Jessica* (1981, revised 1986), created in a complex collaboration with Métis artist and activist Maria Campbell, she waded into some of the most important and explosive debates in contemporary Canadian arts and society, provoking—even personifying—key questions around the representation of Indigeneity, the ongoing impact of settler colonialism, and the problem of cultural appropriation. In works such as *The Darling Family* (1991), *The Duchess* (1998), and *The Age of Arousal* (2007), she cast a searching and sometimes controversial eye on the relations between and within genders. As a key performer in many of her own plays, she embodied ideas and questions in scintillating, troubling, challenging style. One of the truly unforgettable figures of contemporary Canadian theatre history, Griffiths both invites and merits the close critical attention that Jacqueline Petropoulos and her contributors have lavished upon her in what I hope will be the first of many collections dedicated to her work.

Upcoming volumes in NECT will explore such timely topics as theatre and (im)migration, dance and dance studies in Canada, and digital theatre, among others. In each of them, the editors hope to follow the series's original vision of opening new vistas in Canadian theatre and performance studies.

In a tribute after Linda Griffiths's death, Annie Gibson, the publisher of this volume, described her in *Quill and Quire* as "a passionate and fearless artist" (Beattie). Taking up the challenge offered by so many artists who, like Griffiths, merit stronger representation in scholarly conversations, NECT aims to offer a similarly passionate and fearless discussion of the possibilities facing Canadian performance as it carries its complicated past into a contested, inviting, and challenging future.

ACKNOWLEDGEMENTS

I would like to acknowledge the many people who contributed to the making of this book. I am very grateful to series editor Roberta Barker for her tremendous patience, guidance, and support as well as her thoughtful advice and attention to detail. My sincere thanks to Annie Gibson and Blake Sproule at Playwrights Canada Press for their commitment and dedication to this project. My work on this publication was supported by a Major Research Grant from York University. I am also deeply indebted to all of the contributors who gave generously and patiently of their time and energy. Without them this collection would not exist.

I would like to thank Robert Wallace for being a trusted mentor and inspiring me to undertake this endeavour. I am also very grateful to Eva Karpinski, Kelli Deeth, and William Gleberzon for believing in this project and encouraging me along the way. Last but not least, my deep thanks to my family for their love and support.

GIVING WOMEN CENTRE STAGE: CELEBRATING THE LIFE AND WORK OF LINDA GRIFFITHS

JACQUELINE PETROPOULOS

A fearless creator with a heart big enough to hold the whole country. A passionate and completely unsentimental Canadian with a mind so sharp she could take on all the big boys at their own game—arts or politics.

—Paul Thompson (qtd. in Pat Donnelly)

These words from the influential theatre director fondly recall the rebellious spirit and creative genius of playwright Linda Griffiths. Today Griffiths is known not only for creating some of the most memorable and successful plays of her generation, but for the originality and breadth of her work, which spanned more than three decades. Throughout this time she worked tirelessly and passionately to redefine theatre in Canada, constantly pushing artistic boundaries in her quest to tell innovative and unconventional stories about Canadians and women.

As both performer and playwright, Griffiths was undoubtedly a trailblazer for women in Canadian theatre. An Anglo-Canadian born in Montreal in 1953, she made her mark early on, becoming part of the burgeoning alternative theatre scene at the age of twenty-one when she joined the newly established 25th Street Theatre in Saskatoon. As a member of the collectives that created *The West Show* and *Paper Wheat*, among others, she worked on some of the most iconic plays of the period, which launched a new era of Canadian drama devoted to nationalist content. This early phase of her career also began a productive period of collaboration with Paul Thompson, who was linked to the company through a network of institutions that included

Theatre Passe Muraille. Known for his unique brand of collective creation, which swept the nation during the 1970s, Thompson took an improvisational approach to playmaking that greatly influenced Griffiths. She used these techniques to write her own plays in the decades that followed, beginning with her breakaway hit *Maggie and Pierre*, written in collaboration with Thompson in 1980. Originally produced at Theatre Passe Muraille, this play catapulted her to fame, touring all the major theatre centres in Canada and also playing New York. Its impact was so far-reaching that Daniel Brooks and Daniel MacIvor recently counted it as one of "the 14 plays that changed everything for Canadian theatre."

Maggie and Pierre quickly established Griffiths as a playwright in her own right and launched the next phase of her career. She never became a conventional writer, often collaborating with others and using improvisation as a tool for creating character and dialogue. All of her early plays from the 1980s were collaborations, and two of the three were improvised;[1] she did not write a play on her own until *The Darling Family* in 1991. This was her first foray into traditional playwriting, since she composed it herself on paper. With the exception of *A Game of Inches*, which returned to the improvisational-collaborative model, all of her subsequent plays in the 1990s and 2000s were authored by Griffiths alone, though she continued to vacillate between writing "on her feet," as she put it, and "paper writing," as well as exploring some variations in between these two poles depending on the nature of the subject matter she wished to explore (Griffiths and Gallagher 126). This unique and hybrid process, which she once referred to as a split personality (Rudakoff 26) and later as a form of bilingualism (Griffiths and Gallagher 126), effectively blurred the boundaries between performance and playwriting, leading to an

---

1   *Maggie and Pierre* and *Jessica* were both collaborations that were based on Griffiths's improvisations, whereas *O.D. on Paradise* was co-written on a computer with Patrick Brymer.

eclectic body of work that reflected her dynamic and constantly fluctuating approach to playwriting.[2]

While it would be impossible to group Griffiths's diverse canon of plays under a singular thread or theme, some noticeable trends stand out in her work. Beginning with Margaret Trudeau, the irrepressible "flower child" who shocked the nation when she turned her back on marriage and motherhood to party with the Rolling Stones on the eve of her famous husband's election night, Griffiths often wrote about bold and unconventional women who defied social norms: the infamous American divorcée portrayed in *The Duchess: AKA Wallis Simpson*, whose passionate love affair with Edward VIII scandalized the world, forcing him to abdicate the throne; the iconoclastic Canadian poet who sacrificed social convention and economic comfort for her art in *Alien Creature: a visitation from Gwendolyn MacEwen*; and "the odd women" who fought against restrictive and repressive Victorian gender norms in *Age of Arousal*. Griffiths also tackled a number of complex feminist issues in her work, including abortion and the contemporary struggle for women's reproductive rights in *The Darling Family*; the sexual, social, and psychological impact of chronic fatigue syndrome, a disease that disproportionately affects middle-aged women, in *Chronic*; and the modern woman's quest for economic and sexual rights in *Age of Arousal*. *Jessica* also depicts a feminist search for identity and female empowerment, though the play ultimately links this motif to the larger struggle of reclaiming a Métis cultural identity for a protagonist who has to fight both racism and sexism in order to regain her power and independence. Interestingly, this shift toward feminist narratives parallels Griffiths's own career trajectory as an aspiring young actress who made her mark during a period that scholars now view as male-dominated

---

2   Griffiths eventually adopted the term "visceral playwriting" to describe her theatrical process: a term that highlights the embodied, performative nature of her improvisational writing as an alternative to traditional "script" writing.

(Levin x), beating "the big boys at their own game," as Thompson puts it, and eventually taking centre stage for herself.[3]

While this focus on gender is a recurring social and political theme in Griffiths's work, it is just one of many issues that she explores in her plays. In her essay for this anthology, Shelley Scott discusses Griffiths's equally strong interest in communal identity and belonging. Comparing the representation of online gaming in *Games: Who Wants to Play?* to the allegorical depiction of warring theatrical clans in *Spiral Woman and The Dirty Theatre*, Scott argues that Griffiths often writes about characters searching for a sense of group solidarity. In an earlier draft of her essay, Scott elaborates on the prevalence of this theme in Griffiths's plays:

> [T]his interest in belonging to a clan or team of some kind takes a form similar to online gaming, through the expression of a shared passion: the sport of baseball in *A Game of Inches* and the television program *Star Trek: The Next Generation* in *Brother Andre's Heart*. In these benign examples, we see that Griffiths appreciates the special appeal of fandom, the shared sense of identity and insider status that is based on esoteric knowledge.[4]

Though Scott focuses on fandom in these instances, Griffiths's preoccupation with group identity could also be extended to the political realm to include her interest in gender representation and her exploration of cultural nationalism.

---

3   In an interview with Kathleen Gallagher, Griffiths says she "felt voiceless" when she first joined 25th Street Theatre, which she "think[s] was [due to] gender," but she quickly found her own voice and discovered she could compete with the men in the room (116–17). This commentary echoes both Thompson's quote and Layne Coleman's piece in this anthology, titled, "Linda Did Not Want to be a Boy, but She Wanted Their Stage Time," which discusses how Griffiths would go on to take centre stage for women.

4   My sincere thanks to Scott for drawing my attention to this important theme in Griffiths's plays, and for allowing me to cite from an unpublished draft of her essay for this anthology.

This notion of a shared sense of identity parallels, but also serves as a departure from, Griffiths's nationalist phase in the 1970s. During this period many theatre artists embraced the label "Canadian" as an oppositional site of cultural identity and belonging that protested the lack of homegrown content in mainstream theatrical institutions (hence the label "alternative" theatre). For its practitioners and supporters, "Canadian theatre" was a counterculture like the ones that Griffiths would write about in her later plays. In *Spiral Woman and The Dirty Theatre* she makes this connection explicit, since the protagonist, who is clearly a stand-in for the playwright, represents Griffiths's own community of theatre professionals who embrace a sense of national pride despite resistance from warring theatre clans. When Griffiths later turned her attention to gender politics and fan-based subcultures, she entered a post-nationalist phase of her career where group identity was no longer defined by national belonging. This shift was in keeping with the larger changes that took place in the Canadian theatre during the mid-to-late 1980s, when the notion of an all-encompassing national identity was critiqued by marginalized and under-represented groups. Indeed, Griffiths would later comment that the success of her plays to a large extent depended on their being "local" (specific to Toronto, as in *Alien Creature*) or non-specific and without "a place name" (as in *The Darling Family*) in order to appeal either to a niche market or a more global one at a time when "Canadian" content was no longer in demand (Griffiths and Gallagher 116).[5]

While she claimed there was no such thing as a quintessential "Griffiths play" because she always chose "specific subjects and . . . specific stories and each one tends to look different," Griffiths nevertheless singled out her use of "the spiritual" and "the fantastical" as a key aspect of her work (Griffiths and Gallagher 120–21). In an interview with Judith Rudakoff in 1990, Griffiths explained that her plays frequently include references to spirituality, as seen in the moment in *Maggie and Pierre* when Pierre gets down on his knees to

---

5   Interestingly, Griffiths also notes that *The Darling Family* has been the most widely produced of all her plays, surpassing even *Maggie and Pierre*, since its lack of specificity makes it more "universal" and thus more appealing to a larger global market (Griffiths and Gallagher 118–19).

pray, the influence of the Rastafarian god Jah and the mysticism surrounding Vic's death in *O.D. on Paradise,* and the depiction of Indigenous spirituality in *Jessica* (18). Griffiths linked this element of her work to magic and fantasy, noting that "fairy tales actually came out of a spiritual tradition, a shared mythological tradition, which is also a psychological tradition" (21). *Spiral Woman and The Dirty Theatre* explicitly dramatizes this connection, since it is written as a fairy tale that puts the protagonist on a spiritual quest to regain her power. Griffiths would continue to explore these concepts in her later work, as seen—for example—in the focus on magic, mythology, and time travel in *Alien Creature* (a title which is itself reminiscent of the sci-fi fantasy genre).[6] In *Brother Andre's Heart* she makes fun of modern-day characters who find themselves divided between fervent Catholicism and an even greater devotion to pop culture. An interest in fairy tales—as seen in the allusions to *Peter Pan* in *The Darling Family* as well as the "mock . . . looking-glass world of Faerie, with foppish aristocrats and dancing jewels" in *The Duchess*—likewise adds to the sense of the fantastical in her work (Wasserman, "Alien" iv). Griffiths's depiction of online gaming culture in *Games: Who Wants to Play?*, one of her last plays to be produced, once again returns to this theme of fantasy.

This emphasis on the surreal and the fantastic is also characteristic of Griffiths's bold experimentation with genre. Having learned the tools of her trade in the most unconventional of ways, when collective creation was revolutionizing both the form and the content of theatre in Canada, Griffiths continued to push the boundaries of genre, often opting for what she called an epic, fantastical, and non-naturalistic style. She also imaginatively blurred the lines between history, biography, and fiction in her works, adamantly refusing to call her plays biographical, though she claimed to "have written more plays inspired by real people than any other Canadian playwright" ("I Am a Thief" 301). While the majority of her plays contain some non-naturalistic

---

6   Picking up on the full title of this play, *Alien Creature: a visitation from Gwendolyn MacEwen,* Jerry Wasserman argues "almost every play [by Griffiths] features some kind of 'alien' invasion or visitation." Noting that the Virus in *Chronic* is one such example, he goes on to explain that many of Griffiths's plays depict "a female protagonist who is wrestling with or channeling the power of some other dimension" ("Alien" iii).

elements, it would be impossible to group them all together, since her style is as eclectic as her choice of subject matter. As director Jackie Maxwell puts it, "Linda was a theatrical pioneer and an adventurer. She passionately believed that theatre is not just telling stories, but finding the perfect and very likely as yet undiscovered way of telling each one" (qtd. in Nestruck).

This passion that Maxwell speaks of—Griffiths's unwavering commitment to her craft—characterized all of her work, right until the end. Shortly after her tragic death from breast cancer in 2014 at the age of sixty-one, MacIvor explained that "Linda was giving notes from the hospice" when the cast for his Halifax production of *Heaven Above, Heaven Below* flew to Toronto "to read for her in the palliative ward" (qtd. in Nestruck). This strong devotion to the theatre was evident early on, when she chose to stay in Canada to hone her art rather than pursue an acting career south of the border. As MacIvor notes in his piece for this anthology, "she . . . was Maggie, and she was Pierre, and she was Lianna [in director John Sayles's 1983 film], and she was a hot ticket in New York, and she could have been a movie star but she came back home to work." "She was a patriot" and "a hero," according to MacIvor, because she ultimately dedicated herself to the creation of innovative new work for stages across the country. Though her untimely death has left a deeply felt absence in Canada's theatre community, her plays continue to be produced around the world: a testimony to their vitality and versatility, and to the profound theatrical legacy she leaves behind.

Despite her unwavering commitment to the development of Canadian drama, Griffiths's plays have received very little scholarly recognition. With the exception of the many studies of *The Book of Jessica*, there have been very few academic articles written about Griffiths, covering only a small portion of her dramatic canon. To date, there have been no full-length studies. This gap in scholarship is surprising, given the fact her work has been so highly celebrated, earning her five Dora Mavor Moore Awards for *Maggie and Pierre* (1980), *O.D. on Paradise* (1983), *Jessica* (1986), and *Alien Creature* (2000); two Chalmers Awards for *Jessica* and *Alien Creature*; a Quinzaine Festival Award for *Jessica*; the Betty Mitchell Award for Best New Play for *Age of Arousal* (2009); a Gemini; and an ACTRA Award for her performance in *Empire Inc.*

(1984). She was twice nominated for the Governor General's Literary Award for *The Darling Family* (1991) and *Alien Creature*. In 2013 she received a Lifetime Membership Award from the Playwrights Guild of Canada, and in 2015 the city of Toronto named the alley adjacent to Theatre Passe Muraille Linda Griffiths Lane to commemorate her rich artistic legacy at this important Canadian institution. There is also a Linda Griffiths Stairwell inside the theatre honouring her memory.

This anthology sets out to fill at least some of the gap in scholarship about Griffiths, celebrating the theatrical legacy of a playwright whose work has not yet received the critical attention it deserves by bringing together literary and theatrical scholars as well as prominent theatre artists who worked with Griffiths. These authors comment on a range of important topics, such as Griffiths's unique creative process, the relationship between her life and her art, and her wide and complex use of literary, historical, and biographical sources. By providing important critical, literary, historical, and personal contexts for understanding her writing, these essays shed new light on Griffiths's plays and the dedicated and talented woman who created them.

The personal essays from Griffiths's close friends and collaborators frame the academic papers, which are divided into two sections. The anthology's first half focuses on Griffiths's relationship and response to her sources. Penny Farfan discusses Griffiths's resistance to categorizing *Age of Arousal* as an adaptation of George Gissing's Victorian novel *The Odd Women*, even though she admits her play was "wildly inspired" by it ("Playwright's Note" 8–9). Arguing that this ambivalence likely stems from traditional views of adaptation as derivative and inferior, Farfan suggests that Linda Hutcheon's alternative theory of adaptation "as a 'palimpsestic' art that acknowledges the source text but is also inevitably a departure from it . . . resonates with Griffiths's description of her work on *Age of Arousal* as involving thievery and creativity." In particular, Farfan reads Griffiths's use of time travel and the foregrounding of sexuality (through the representation of lesbian, transgender, "multi-amorous," and "free love" characters) as significant departures from the source text that nevertheless pay homage to *The Odd Women* by pointing to the hidden possibilities within the text that were unspeakable in Gissing's own time. Farfan goes on to argue that this reworking of her literary source, through the celebration of multiple sexualities and the shifting of chronologies to include modern and contemporary concerns, allows Griffiths to connect feminist histories of the past to a more "utopian" future that she imagines for twenty-first century feminisms.

Brent Wood also examines Griffiths's historical and literary sources in his discussion of *Alien Creature*, drawing attention to the play's complex interweaving of biographical material with poetic lines and imagery from MacEwen's work. By carefully unpacking the many literary allusions explored in *Alien Creature*—derived from MacEwen's obsession with death, war, and darkness, as well as her love of mythology, magic, and comic books—Wood provides a compelling reading of the ways in which these images reflect both the protagonist's mental suffering and tragic decline as well as her spiritual longing for other worlds and dimensions as a form of transcendence. He shows us, moreover, how powerfully Griffiths draws upon the theatrical motif of the magic show as the central metaphor of the play, ultimately depicting "MacEwen's story as a tragedy in which faith in magic fails to halt the heroine's downfall yet offers a hint of redemption in a flicker of ghostly light."

Ann Wilson also examines Griffiths's use of intertextuality and her interest in the world of make-believe by considering the question of why she named *The Darling Family* after the family in *Peter Pan*, a classic children's play that was later made into a famous Disney cartoon. By linking this literary source to the play's representation of spirituality and memories of a past life, this essay provides yet another example of Griffiths's preoccupation with other worlds and dimensions in her work. Wilson argues that the textual "references to J.M. Barrie's *Peter Pan* serve as subtle, but consistent, reminders that a play is artifice, a medium that is characterized by pretending." This, in turn, allows Griffiths to explore the issue of how truth is constituted in the theatre. According to Wilson, "Rather than a character speaking the 'truth' or actors finding the 'truth' of their character, Griffiths's play suggests that 'truth' in the theatre is primarily constituted in two interrelated ways: the trust between actors that allows the action to seem real, and the audience believing in the veracity of the action unfolding on the stage." The simplicity of *The Darling*

Family, which pares theatre down to a minimalist set and two actors on stage, likewise enables Griffiths to explore this metatheatrical theme.

Sherrill Grace's essay closes this section on sources by comparing *The Duchess: AKA Wallis Simpson* to Timothy Findley's *Famous Last Words*, arguing that the striking similarities between them suggest Griffiths may have "read Findley's novel, as well as some of the same [historical and biographical] sources he consulted." Like Wood and Wilson, Grace comments on the metatheatrical and fantastical aspects of Griffiths's work; her essay also introduces the key preoccupations of the volume's second half: memory, process, and selfhood. Both *The Duchess* and *Famous Last Words* focus on memory and performance as key structural devices and metaphors for their reinventions of Wallis Simpson. "Despite the similarities, however, there are some key differences in these portraits," according to Grace, "most importantly in the ethical dimensions of the texts and the characterization of Wallis." Unlike Findley's novel, which explores competing views of historical events, Griffiths's "memory play within the play is staged as a '[f]airy-tale romance' . . . with Wallis as the self-styled 'Faerie Queene.'" By focusing primarily on the main character of the play, Griffiths paints a picture of an ambitious woman who was unfairly condemned by society for not adhering to gender roles. Though *The Duchess* touches on some of the negative aspects of Wallis's character, Griffiths's examination of the sexism of the early twentieth century humanizes the play's protagonist by depicting her as a controversial historical figure "who refuses to be a victim or succumb to a supporting role in her husband's life or accept her public image as merely gaudy spectacle."

Amanda Attrell's essay continues to explore the question of Griffiths's use of biographical material and her interest in concepts such as memory and metatheatre while also introducing the focus of the second half of the anthology: Griffiths's unique and multi-faceted creative process and her interest in the representation of identity. By looking at the development of *The Last Dog of War* during the period in which it was workshopped and rewritten, Attrell argues that this text began as a historical and biographical play about her father's time as a World War II pilot but became increasingly more personal and autobiographical with each new revision of the script, eventually providing a portrait of the playwright herself. While Griffiths is better known for working with historical, biographical, and literary sources, she draws on deeply personal and familial memories in *The Last Dog of War*, leading to the construction of an autobiographical self that changed with each new performance in response to the relationship between Griffiths and her audiences. This theatrical process is embedded in the play itself, Attrell argues, since the script comments on its own creation by emphasizing the fact "that all of the roles in the play—playwright, performer, characters, and audience members—have been in flux throughout the development of Griffiths's autobiographical self."

I also explore Griffiths's artistic process and her personal relationship to her work by examining *The Book of Jessica: A Theatrical Transformation*. This text explicitly addresses the question of theatrical process in its discussion of the making of *Jessica*, a play based on the life experiences and autobiography of Maria Campbell. In this essay I consider the shifting social, political, and cultural contexts that shaped critical interpretations of both *Jessica* and *The Book of Jessica*. I argue that *Jessica* was originally celebrated as a truthful representation of identity by the mainstream press due to the rise of visibility politics in the 1980s, but this reading was later challenged by the charges of cultural appropriation that surfaced with the publication of *The Book of Jessica* by Griffiths and Campbell in 1989. While scholars initially criticized Griffiths for reinscribing the colonialist strategies the book set out to critique, this view has since been problematized by new theories of collaborative writing as a practice that confronts relations of power and difference between subjects who are not always equal. This critical approach provides a useful framework for re-examining the play *Jessica* as a shared, but conflicted, site of cross-cultural collaboration between white and Indigenous theatre artists.

Shelley Scott's paper concludes the second half of the anthology devoted to the question of theatrical process and the representation of identity. She also revisits the motif of fantasy explored in the first section of essays. Scott examines the multi-staged development process behind the creation of one of Griffiths's final productions, *Games: Who Wants to Play?* She considers

Griffiths's workshops in "visceral playwriting" exploring the topic of gaming culture with students at University of Lethbridge, as well as the different iterations, and evolution, of this theme from the earlier drafts of the play to its final published version. Written near the end of her life, in the period between 2010–2014, *Games* appears on the surface to be a significant departure for Griffiths due to its focus on the male adolescent obsession with gaming, a world she admitted she knew little about. However, Scott argues that the play probes many issues central to Griffiths's canon, such as "her fascination with fantasy, group identity, and belonging."

In addition to providing new critical interpretations of Griffiths's plays, this collection also includes personal essays from influential theatre artists who worked closely with Griffiths throughout her life. These pieces from Paul Thompson, Daniel MacIvor, and Layne Coleman help to frame the anthology, providing important insights into Griffiths's career trajectory.

Thompson's essay, "The Road to Becoming a Writer," traces Griffiths's inspiring journey from collective playmaking and improvisational theatre in the 1970s to her transformation into a playwright in the 1980s. Thompson, who worked closely with Griffiths during this period, provides many compelling anecdotes and insights into her creative process and the milestones that helped shape her career as both a performer and writer. His essay also paints a clear picture of Griffiths's transition from an improvisational actor to a playwright who would one day require "a room of her own" as Thompson puts it, alluding to Virginia Woolf's landmark study of women writers.

MacIvor's essay "Who Is She?" provides (as he notes in the subtitle) "A Subjective Assemblage on Linda G." Weaving together personal anecdotes about Griffiths, their friendship, and their work together on *The Last Dog of War*, as well as his own personal reflections on the many plays and performances by Griffiths he witnessed over the years, MacIvor offers profound insights into her dramatic oeuvre as seen through the eyes of a fellow performer and playwright with a keen sense of the inner mechanics of writing for the theatre.

In his paper "Linda Did Not Want to be a Boy, but She Wanted Their Stage Time," Coleman shares his personal recollections of what it was like to work with Griffiths, focusing in particular on their time together at 25th Street Theatre, which he describes as one of the happiest and most exhilarating periods of her life. Coleman's deeply moving and reflective piece pays homage to Griffiths's indomitable spirit and her remarkable dedication to a life of arts and letters. He also commends her for writing "plays that are being done around the world, telling stories that give women centre stage."

This anthology performs the academic equivalent of giving Griffiths centre stage. In so doing it celebrates her many achievements as a woman who broke through gender barriers to become one of the most successful dramatists in Canada. Since her plays continue to attract audiences around the world, this anthology is surely only the start of a long overdue conversation about Griffiths's significant body of work. As such, it stands as both a tribute to the power of her art and a testimony to her impressive legacy as a performer and playwright who for decades stood at the forefront of theatrical innovation in Canada.

THE ROAD TO BECOMING A WRITER

PAUL THOMPSON

Linda Griffiths was kicked out of the acting program at the National Theatre of Canada because she couldn't improvise. This obviously painful moment became a standing joke during our seven-year period of making collective plays together at Theatre Passe Muraille (TPM). Because the one thing that Linda could do better than pretty well anybody else in whatever room we found ourselves was IMPROVISE.

I first met Linda in Saskatoon in the summer of '75. I had brought a full team of Passe Muraille veterans to work on a challenging piece to be called *The West Show*. Linda was part of a talented young company, 25th Street Theatre, with a one hundred–seat space that remains one of the best rooms for making plays I can remember. Ironically, it wasn't on 25th Street. In exchange for free rent I would pass on the techniques of our collective to the company and we would make a play named *If You're So Good, Why Are You In Saskatoon?* The process was pretty straightforward: the first half of the day I spent with TPM actors, who would then go out scouring the city and surrounding parts of the province as research, and the second half of the day and into the evening I spent with the home company.

There is a moment in the early life of a theatre company when anything seems possible. This for me was the 25th company in the summer of 1975. In the middle of it all Linda embracing all the things that it was permitted to imagine and perform on a stage. Now this was a group that would give our country two artistic directors, four playwrights, and four very full acting careers.[1] But here, imagine Linda with these first discoveries. It was like watching a painter with an entirely new set of pigments. Linda would talk of her breakthrough as being her incidental role in a drive-in movie sequence where she acted out all of *Jaws* for the couple in the car and finally had to be hauled off the stage.[2] My preference was a later moment in a part of the play that became "The Spirit of the Bessborough Gardens"—a neo-Gothic retreat complete with gargoyles—where Linda absorbed landscape, history, and the spiritual dimension into the most compelling sequence of the play. From this point forward transcendence would become an integral and defining part of Linda's theatre creations and her life. But let's look further at Linda the actor. She was not yet beautiful and she didn't glide into the lead's story. She opted for the sidekick-of-the-pretty-girl role and shone in incidental character parts. She was gregarious, but at the same time more than a little off-putting with her plaid shirt, unshaven legs, and construction boots. She had, however, a boyfriend named Layne in the company, and she could talk and argue forever into the night in their tiny two-by-four apartment, all of us perched on improvised stools made from off-sale six-packs of beer. We talked about the country, the state of theatre, the world. Linda had a sharp, piercing mind and a wicked laugh and little escaped her notice. It's strange that with all the later obsessions she had with diet and health, my memory has Linda and Karen Wiens going drink for drink with the "boys"; there was never a bottle saved for another evening.

Back in rehearsal these conversations would fuel scenes, create dilemmas, launch characters. Saskatoon was a city vibrant with people on the move and just big enough and ambitious enough to be hungry for its own mythology. An ideal canvas. Linda was always one of the first up with an idea. Her character

---

1   In addition to Linda Griffiths, who become an actor and playwright, Layne Coleman would go on to become artistic director of 25th Street Theatre and Theatre Passe Muraille, an actor, and a playwright; Andy Tahn would go on to become artistic director of 25th Street Theatre; Chris Covert became a playwright; and Karen Wiens and Bob Collins would develop full acting careers.

2   Linda Griffiths gives an excellent account of this in her interview with Andrew Moodie for Theatre Museum Canada. See "Linda Griffiths on Creation."

work was thrilling, for she would find these portraits just a bit deeper in the body, a bit more beyond the brain, so there was always a surprise or unexpected turn. Her characters were hard to forget. And funny. The play didn't start out as a comedy and Linda was dead serious about her acting, but by the end of its heldover runs the play had given her a master class in comedy. Yet perhaps the most enduring gift the show brought was the spirit of engagement with a popular audience. This hunger for complicity with the public haunted all the future plays I made with Linda.

The summer ended and I left to make other shows. Linda played, toured, and replayed 25th Street's hit, then started on the epic that would become *Paper Wheat* (the defining Western collective). Linda would split from the second version of that, act in several "real" plays, work on another collective out west, collaborate with me and my core actors on an ambitious cultural comedy, cameo in another TPM original, and continue her quest as an actor.

The next defining collaboration would take us to Montreal, three years after our first. Again it would be game-changing. The play: *Les Maudits Anglais*. The ambition: create a play in bad French by an Anglo-Canadian cast for a Québécois nationalist (was there any other kind in 1978?) audience. By this point Linda had grown beyond her years—a piece of information she wouldn't disclose even then—and the work together was electric. This was a homecoming for her. So you knew why the stakes were so high. By now she would bring in highly elaborate scenes in different theatre styles, as well as her character work. One example that made it into the play was a Pierrot-inspired clown, complete with whiteface and balloon, that appeared one day in rehearsal unannounced. Her core character was a Ukrainian separatist from Alberta eager to learn from her Montreal counterparts, but the heart of Linda's drive in the play was to find an expression for her own sense of nationalism in response to the Québécois surge. All this in fractured French. She had one speech in the play that was a showstopper every night we played Rue Papineau. Quebecers loved her nerve. And her verve. Linda's character preference still clung to the non-stylish, but a Quebec playwright named Claude, who had been brought on board to make our bad French more palatable, started to tease out Linda's inner beauty, and charmed her into inhabiting the beautiful dress that had been designed. Suddenly she was gorgeous, and the audience would assure her it was true. Scenes are easy; plays are hard. The arguments over the making of the play went on. Linda's intellectual confidence grew and continued to spill into the after-hours. She had a passion to know and an appetite to embrace all aspects of making a play. One thrilling sidebar to, or maybe a product of, all this thinking was a cameo performance that evoked a "frisson" every time I saw it: Linda embodying Pierre Trudeau in all his Jesuitical splendour. It was discomforting and compelling in equal measure.

You would think that with the overwhelming response to our French hit Linda would be eager to go back into the creative room. Far from it. For me this was more than strange. We had a stunning idea and the resources, but it still took Linda well over a year to agree on a one-person *Maggie and Pierre*. Maybe this was the starting point for Linda the writer. Maybe she foresaw how it would take her away from her family of fellow actors. Maybe she didn't really enjoy the spirit of anarchy that seemed an inevitable handmaiden to all my collectives even though she thrived there like few others. Whatever the reasons, she finally agreed to move into the Backspace of Passe Muraille in the late fall of 1979 and we dug in. I remember exceptional research, great imaginative discoveries, early smart moves on collaborative designs. I remember fantastic, seamless riffs by Linda that would go on for more than forty minutes. I remember political arguments and theatre arguments that would jump from stage to audience seats and back. Then spill over into a post-day beer at the Epicure Café. Mainly it was just Linda and me, though design allies and objects would flow through. No retinue for the director, no stage manager for the actor, and nothing was written down. It seemed that the room was the archivist of our experience and nothing was in danger of being lost. We changed the very nature of the play's structure close to half a dozen times and this only seemed to make Linda's performance more brilliant. We stopped the work in the room cold because our political understanding was becoming clichéd. So Linda headed to Ottawa to study an opportune opening of Parliament, and a more opportune dance with Pierre. She returned, fighting for her characters with renewed authority. Finally, there would be three: Margaret, Pierre, and Henry, the journalist, a personage never to have his due. What was wonderful in this development was that Linda could hold the whole play in her mind and in her body while sharing it fully on stage. I remember a complete version that clocked in at two hours and twenty minutes and an early guest audience member detected no repetitions or wanderings in the story. Finally it resolved to its two forty-five minute acts. Still no script, just a map on the wall. The stage manager couldn't use one because he was too busy tracking and effecting the costume changes back stage. Lights and sound decided to treat it like rock and roll.

The play did rock, across the country and back . . . and beyond. But that story is for another time. What we need to try and understand here is what was happening to Linda. Somewhere in here, amidst the huge circus of publicity enveloping the play, there was a writer being formed. Somewhere in this time it must have become very attractive and comforting to imagine Virginia Woolf's "room of one's own." We never talked about it, but I do remember that about that time we started to joke about the needs emanating from Linda the actor and Linda the writer. The play, of course, did get written down, and on the page looked surprisingly like dramatic literature. I'm sure that Linda the writer was more than a bit happy.

If the preamble to *Maggie and Pierre* took more than a year, the buildup for *Jessica* was more like six. To be fair though, Linda was only involved in the last two. I had met Maria Campbell during the summer of 1975 in and around Saskatoon, and she had been very enthusiastic about *The West Show*, in particular Anne Anglin's Métis character's story. Maria was strongly drawn to theatre as a form and felt that the collective might be the right format to tell the parts of her story that hadn't made it into her compelling autobiography *Halfbreed.* She also believed that theatre was the true home for the magical ways that guided her life. The challenge of who should play Maria went on for a long time. It was a collective. Maria didn't act, and we could find no Indigenous actor drawn to the challenge of playing her. Anne Anglin considered it but didn't think she could live in the complex world of this story. The choice fell to Linda, and the challenges of the play *Jessica* have their own book.

But for the purpose of this article it would be useful to note how the lengthy period of research, theatre structure debate, and concern for the moral implications in our choices had started to imprint on Linda's relationship with the theatre. We were back to the arguing of those early nights in Saskatoon. Only now they would go on all day as well, and be picked up the next, and the next. Smart friends uninvolved with the show would be drawn in to make their points. For me, this was the ultimate launch of Linda the writer, a sort of Balzac-like driven need to surround herself with a complete world before finally committing to the play. Of course there were the workshops and they were difficult. Of course there was Tantoo Cardinal and Graham Greene and their extraordinary characters. Of course this hugely challenging project would remain, at least for me, not quite finished. But in the middle of it all was stubborn Linda, smart Linda, vulnerable Linda, pushing it on, massaging the ideas from within the scenes. And finally, actual writing came into the room. Linda, Maria, and me, in the Backspace; a tape recorder; Linda improvising all the scenes. And finally, a script. Paper being allowed into the room of the collective. It would also be the first step for Linda out of this wonderful room of improvisation. It would be scary and more than a bit lonely. But, as Linda the writer, she would have . . . a room of her own.

AGES OF AROUSAL

PENNY FARFAN

Linda Griffiths's *Age of Arousal* (2007) is recognizably based on George Gissing's novel *The Odd Women* (1893), yet she described her play as "wildly inspired" by Gissing's text rather than an adaptation of it ("Playwright's Note" 8–9). Griffiths's resistance to categorizing *Age of Arousal* as an adaptation may be explained in part by her ambivalence about the Merchant Ivory production company's popular movie adaptations of classic British and American novels. Recalling her research process for *Age of Arousal*, she writes of "dreaming [her] way through many hours of perfectly produced costume drama" while "[feeling] guilty at the same time":

> The lack of edge, the sometimes saccharine devotion to form. No matter how well these dramas serve the original authors, it's hard to get a sense of the groundbreaking nature of their work through the mists of time. It all looks so . . . acceptable. I was determined that *Age of Arousal* would blast past reverence into new territory. ("A Flagrantly Weird Age" 137; ellipsis in original)

To recapture something of the original newness of Gissing's novel about the emergence of modern gender roles and related ideas about female sexuality in the late nineteenth century, Griffiths chose to foreground sex in a more explicit way than was possible for Gissing as a writer bound by the social and literary conventions of his time ("Playwright's Note" 10). She also wanted to correct some residual misogyny that she perceived in Gissing's text, despite his extraordinary accomplishment in portraying so many central female

characters together in a single work. In Griffiths's note at the start of the published text of *Age of Arousal*, she describes her approach to Gissing's novel as
"tak[ing] his basic characters and situation and leap[ing] off a cliff" that she
"was dying to leap off." Her writing of *Age of Arousal* was consequently, in her
words, a "dance of thievery and creativity . . . danced with Gissing floating
above, patron saint or appalled spectre" ("Playwright's Note" 8).

In *A Theory of Adaptation*, Linda Hutcheon notes a critical tendency to
view popular adaptations of canonical literary works as "inferior and secondary" to their source texts (4). This paradigm aligns with Griffiths's ambivalence
about Merchant Ivory–style movie adaptations, yet Hutcheon also posits
an alternative view of adaptation that resonates with Griffiths's description
of her work on *Age of Arousal* as involving both thievery and creativity.
Adaptation, Hutcheon argues, is a "palimpsestic" art that acknowledges the
source text but is also inevitably a departure from it (9). An adaptation is thus
double in nature: both "process and product" (9), interpretation and creation,
persistence and change, "repetition without replication" (7), "a derivation
that is not derivative—a work that is second without being secondary" (9).
Approaching "adaptations *as adaptations*" (4; emphasis in original), Hutcheon
proposes, entails engaging this "double nature" (6) and also recognizing that
adaptations pay homage to but may also contest their source texts (20).

While Griffiths resists categorizing *Age of Arousal* as an adaptation in
order to justify her departure from Gissing's novel and differentiate her play
from its source, her program note for the play's premiere at the Enbridge play-
Rites Festival of New Canadian Plays at Alberta Theatre Projects in Calgary
in 2007, and also the substantial playwright's note and research essay with
which she chose to frame the published text, make clear that the play is in fact
an adaptation in precisely the double sense that Hutcheon theorizes. In this
essay, I resist Griffiths's resistance to categorizing *Age of Arousal* as an adaptation and instead, following Hutcheon, approach the play *as* an adaptation
in order to understand it as at once an interpretation of a prior text and a distinct creation in its own right. Expanding on Griffiths's claim that her primary
intervention in relation to *The Odd Women* was to add "the element of sex,"
about which Victorian standards of decorum precluded explicit discourse

for both Gissing and his characters ("Playwright's Note" 10), I reflect more broadly on how her play plays with time, and particularly with feminism's times. Exemplary of the double nature that Hutcheon identifies as fundamental to adaptations, Griffiths's adaptation revisits Gissing's novel through what she calls her "time travel" ("A Flagrantly Weird Age" 136–37) across several key "ages of arousal" in the interlinked personal and political senses definitive of feminism. In doing so, the play raises questions about the status and future of feminism in Griffiths's own present/historical moment circa 2007 and about Griffiths herself as the interpreter/creator of *Age of Arousal*, an adaptation of a canonical nineteenth-century text. As an adaptation, I argue, *Age of Arousal* is thus palimpsestic not only in its relation to *The Odd Women* but also in its relation to the history of feminism.

The Odd Women is one of a cluster of British "New Woman" novels of the 1890s that arose in response to a historical moment when women were believed to outnumber men and those who were unpaired with a husband were perceived as "superfluous" (Ingham vii) or—in Gissing's words about the central characters of his novel—"*odd* in the sense that they do not make a match; as we say 'an odd glove'" (qtd. in Showalter 19). The idea of the "odd woman" was closely related to the emergence of the cultural figure of the so-called "New Woman" in the 1880s and 1890s, a period of what Gissing regarded as "sexual anarchy" during which unmarried middle-class women upset the prevailing social order as they began to experience financial independence through employment outside the home and, with it, greater personal autonomy (qtd. in Ingham xvii, and Showalter 3). The "oddness" of being unpaired with a husband and thus outside the ideal of middle-class womanhood (Ingham vii) took on sexual resonances as unmarried women explored alternative relationships beyond the bounds of heterosexual marriage and the patriarchal nuclear family.

In Gissing's novel, Mary Barfoot and Rhoda Nunn are cohabiting friends and colleagues who together operate a school that provides professional training, including typewriting, to unmarried middle-class women experiencing financial difficulties. The return of Mary's cousin Everard from abroad complicates Mary and Rhoda's relationship, awakening in the younger and financially less secure Rhoda a romantic desire that threatens to unsettle her commitment to exemplifying for her "odd women" students the possibility of leading a fulfilling life outside of marriage.[1] Everard is attracted to Rhoda because her progressive thinking as a New Woman makes her not only a more interesting female companion but also a more challenging sexual conquest, particularly given her "nun"-like aspects. Over the course of the novel, his attachment to Rhoda develops to the point that he proposes to her, initially suggesting a free union to test the completeness of her devotion to him and then revising his offer to legal marriage. Everard and Rhoda's efforts to form an ideal relationship are complicated, however, by their own ingrained concerns about power, dominance, and trust between men and women, and these concerns are intensified by a secondary plot line arising from Rhoda's offer to provide secretarial training to three acquaintances from childhood, the unmarried sisters Alice, Virginia, and Monica Madden, who have fallen on hard financial times following the death of their father. The Madden sisters prove to be less-than-ideal students, particularly Monica, the youngest and prettiest of the three and therefore the one with the best prospects of marriage. Monica marries securely but unhappily and falls into an illicit relationship with another man before realizing her misjudgment of her lover's character and also that she is pregnant by her husband. Through an unfortunate chance, Everard is mistakenly presumed by Rhoda to be Monica's lover, but he refuses to prove his innocence, demanding instead that Rhoda trust him completely. Monica, soon to die in childbirth, clears Everard of any part in her downfall, yet Rhoda still finds herself unable to trust him fully or to see how their relationship can match her ideal, whether within or outside of the institution of marriage. Their relationship ends, and at the close of the novel, Rhoda, now forever "odd" but flourishing in her work, cradles Monica's orphaned daughter, who has been left by her father to be raised by her aunts. In the novel's final sentence, Rhoda, having seen something of Monica in the baby's eyes, murmurs, "Poor little child" (371). Patricia Ingham has likened *The Odd Women* to a maze

---

1   As Rhoda says, "My work involves not just teaching but *being* an odd woman" (*Age of Arousal* 99).

that winds its way through the intersections of gender, sexuality, and class as they play out in relation to the institution of marriage, arguing that while the novel ends in an impasse on every issue it confronts, "[t]he impasse reflects not stasis but turbulence out of which change can result" (xix). The ideal relationship of equality and trust between man and woman—what Nora in Henrik Ibsen's foundational "New Woman" play *A Doll's House* (1879) refers to as "the miracle of miracles" (86)—remains in the future.

In *Age of Arousal*, Griffiths reduces Gissing's larger cast of characters to six—Rhoda, Mary, Everard, Monica, Virginia, and Alice—dropping Monica's husband, along with a number of minor characters and subplots that echo the novel's main plots and themes. Foregrounding sexuality to create what Jerry Wasserman has called "an erotic portrait of a turbulent era" ("Linda" 387), Griffiths also transforms the homosocial relationship between Mary and Rhoda into a lesbian one; makes Everard a gynecologist rather than an engineer and involves him in a sexual relationship with Monica; portrays Monica as a "multi-amorous" pioneer of "free lovism" who embarks on a personal campaign for "erotical freedoms" that is doomed by the lack of adequate birth control (*Age of Arousal* 93, 94, 82); and has Virginia travel to Germany—hotbed of early sexology research, including on transvestism[2]— where she discovers freedom in cross-dressing and communing with other cross-dressing women, gaining control of her alcoholism until she returns to England and resumes dressing as a woman in compliance with conventional

---

2   German sexologist and homosexual rights advocate Magnus Hirschfeld (1868–1935), for example, did extensive research on "the third sex" and "sexual inversion" and is credited with having coined the term *transvestism* (Weeks 129). In *Age of Arousal*, Everard and Rhoda discuss the new science of sexology (68) and Virginia reveals that she got the idea of going to Berlin to "learn to smoke and wear trousers" from pamphlets in Mary and Rhoda's house (75–76). These references to sexology may be another dimension of Griffiths's "time travel," given that the field of sexology was still in its earliest stages in 1885 when *Age of Arousal* is set. Karl Heinrich Ulrichs's studies had by then been published, but Hirschfeld's work in the field began in the 1890s, as did that of British sexologist Havelock Ellis. Richard von Krafft-Ebing's *Psychopathia Sexualis* was published in German in 1886.

expectations regarding gender and sexuality.[3] Even readers and spectators who are not familiar with the plot and characters of *The Odd Women* will recognize the departure of *Age of Arousal* from Victorian literary convention through Griffiths's use of what she calls "thoughtspeak"—essentially giving voice to the subtext as she extrapolates it from Gissing or invents it herself, often articulating sexual content unspeakable in the characters' social context, where decorum is crucial, as it was in Gissing's own literary-historical moment as a writer. These "wild uncensored outpourings" (Griffiths, "Playwright's Note" 13) register as anachronistic, yet at the same time, despite being more explicit than was possible for Gissing and his characters, they retain traces of the original historical context of the novel, for example, through the use of quaint and comical terms like "doodle" and "quim" for male and female genitals respectively (Griffiths, *Age of Arousal* 60, 93).

While such changes foreground "the element of sex" that Griffiths identified as her key intervention in adapting Gissing's novel, her most significant revision may in fact be the time in which she chose to set her play. *Age of Arousal* takes place in 1885, yet the play's opening scene, entitled "The Dream," establishes sixty-year-old Mary Barfoot as a former suffragist who is haunted by her past experience of forced feeding to end her hunger strike during

---

3   Griffiths's Virginia discovers in Berlin that she wants "to be a woman, yet dress as a man" (111), but she remains uncertain about her sexual identity due to her fear of transgressing heterosexual norms. Explaining to her sister Alice why she returned to London, Virginia recalls, in a striking passage, an aborted moment of sexual contact with one of her Berlin friends:

> One night I shared a bed with one of them, which we often did for sisterly economy, but this night she reached out for me, I do not know what I felt, will never know, for I began to gasp. I looked down at the locket with Mother and Father's hair intertwined and saw the hair was growing out of the locket 'round my heart, then around my throat, pulling tight, strangling me, Mother and Father and yes, you Alice and Monica were above me calling to me that I had betrayed you and as I lay there I knew it was so. I found myself beating my friend, my hands squeezing, throttling her neck, I nearly killed her. I left on the next train. (110)

Humber & University of Guelph-Humber Library

0134150109422

her imprisonment for militant suffrage activism and who has retreated from direct political struggle to found her school for women. In the "Time Travel" section of her essay on her research for the play, Griffiths explains that "[i]n *Age of Arousal*, time is collapsed, inverted, stomped on, in an effort to straddle important points in Britain's struggle for women's rights. It's all true, just rearranged. The play is set in 1885. The time period that encompasses all aspects of the play is from 1869 to 1914. Forty-five years." Adding that while "the militant feminist movement . . . arguably began with the first arrest in 1905," she explains that she wanted her play to be "set in deep Victoriana," with "the fusty velvets, the tight corsets, the claustrophobia of a world about to ignite," so that "a blast of modernity" would "come from underneath the dust bunnies of Victorian England" ("A Flagrantly Weird Age" 136). Mary's dream of her prison experience is thus in a larger sense Griffiths's own "idea" or "dream of Victorian England"—a "fabulist construct" or fantasy premised on Gissing's text yet comparable in its time-travelling to science fiction (Griffiths, "Playwright's Note" 12, 10–11). Griffiths's revision of historical chronology links her seemingly primary focus on "the sexual lives of the women" in *Age of Arousal* ("A Flagrantly Weird Age" 138) to the history of feminism, opening onto larger questions about the status of feminism not only in the late nineteenth and early twentieth centuries but also at the time of her adaptation of Gissing's novel in the early twenty-first century.

In theorizing adaptation, Hutcheon draws on the scientific analogy of Darwinian evolution, "where genetic adaptation is presented as the biological process by which something is fitted to a given environment." In doing so, Hutcheon proposes "think[ing] of narrative adaptation in terms of a story's fit and its process of mutation or adjustment, through adaptation, to a particular cultural environment." As she explains, "Stories also evolve by adaptation and are not immutable over time. Sometimes, like biological adaptation, cultural adaptation involves migration to favorable conditions: stories travel to different cultures and different media. In short, stories adapt just as they are adapted" (31). In *Adaptation and Appropriation*, Julie Sanders similarly likens the transformation of source texts through the process of adaptation to a kind of genetic adaptation (12). She notes, moreover, that adaptations are often motivated or influenced "by movements in, and readings produced by, the theoretical and intellectual arena as much as by their so-called sources" (13), and she lists feminist and queer theory among other critical developments informing contemporary adaptations. Sanders's observation resonates with Griffiths's remark that as she worked on *Age of Arousal*, her "research on the women's suffrage movement and the Victorian age took precedence" over Gissing's novel, which she began deliberately to avoid, "refusing to read it again" ("Playwright's Note" 9).

It is certainly unusual for a play to include not only a lengthy playwright's note but a research essay and an annotated bibliography of suggested titles for further reading, yet that is how Griffiths chose to frame the published text of *Age of Arousal*. Her research essay ranges across such topics as Victorian gender norms and sexual ideology, the institution of marriage, spinsters and lesbians, the male-dominated medical profession, and the suffrage movement, and while her bibliography includes male-authored cultural studies such as Steven Marcus's *The Other Victorians: A Study of Sexuality and Pornography in Mid-Nineteenth-Century England*, it is most heavily weighted toward feminist historiography of the 1970s and 1980s. For example, Susan Kingsley Kent's *Sex and Suffrage in Britain 1860–1914* (1987) is identified by Griffiths as a crucial resource for her research ("A Flagrantly Weird Age" 136) and is annotated in her bibliography as follows: "*Without a doubt the most brilliant of all the books I read. A main source for an understanding of feminist thought at the time and the philosophies that opposed them. Especially good on the pre-militant movements of 1860 to 1906* ("Further Reading" 169; italics in original). The bibliography also includes a section on "Modern Theory" (171) by second-wave feminists like Germaine Greer, a few of whose words, Griffiths admits in the notes at the end of her essay ("A Flagrantly Weird Age" 167), were actually incorporated into the dialogue of *Age of Arousal*.[4] Griffiths's

---

4   Griffiths refers to Greer, Betty Friedan, and Kate Millett as "'first-wave' modern feminists" ("A Flagrantly Weird Age" 137), by which she appears to mean that they were the early thinkers of feminism's second wave in the 1960s, '70s, and '80s, the actual first wave being in the late nineteenth and early twentieth centuries and encompassing the campaign for women's suffrage.

restaging of proto- and first-wave feminism in the late nineteenth and early twentieth centuries was thus informed by and filtered through key texts of second-wave feminist historiography and literary and cultural criticism. In this way, her play quite literally reflects Katherine Kelly's observation of "an affinity between the thinking of Western feminist historiographers from the 1970s forward and the creative work of . . . feminist playwrights who have used the drama to 'make the bones sing'"—that is, "to recover the silenced histories of women" and "reimagine women's past lives as a first step toward living a more just present and future" (199). As Griffiths's research process for *Age of Arousal* illustrates, feminist historiography has made women's and feminist history available as "a useable past" for women theatre artists and their audiences in what Kelly describes as "a selective retrieval of past events that, from the vantage point of the present, opened a door—perhaps briefly— on the possibility of building a women's community" (206).

Jerry Wasserman has pointed out that Griffiths was "[o]ne of the few Canadian playwrights to have emerged in the 1970s and remained active well into the twenty-first century" ("Linda" 387). Griffiths might thus be seen to have played a part in the emergence of the second wave of feminism that motivated much of the research that she drew upon in writing *Age of Arousal*. Beyond her acclaimed gender-shifting solo performance *Maggie and Pierre* (1980), about Canadian prime minister Pierre Elliott Trudeau, his wife Margaret Sinclair Trudeau, and a fictional reporter captivated by their relationship, Griffiths's early work included playing the title role in John Sayles's 1983 film *Lianna*, about a woman who leaves her husband when she discovers her lesbian sexuality and who subsequently revels in but also struggles with the social realities of her new identity. Griffiths also performed in celebrated feminist playwright Caryl Churchill's *Fen* at the Public Theater in New York in 1984, and her own later dramatic canon includes a number of plays centring on female characters, most notably *Jessica* (originally developed in 1982 with Maria Campbell and Paul Thompson; revised in 1986), *The Duchess: AKA Wallis Simpson* (1998), and *Alien Creature: a visitation from Gwendolyn MacEwen* (1999).

While *Age of Arousal* is informed by second-wave feminist historiography, theory, and criticism, it was written in the early twenty-first century from the perspective of third-wave feminism. As Kelly states, Griffiths "reimagine[s] the first wave through the revisions of the third, . . . acknowledging lesbian love and attending to class differences that first-wave feminists have been charged with having ignored" (207). Moreover, Kelly argues, by resequencing historical events in *Age of Arousal* so that the suffrage campaign predates "New Woman events from the 1880s, such as the advent of typewriting and independent living for unmarried women," Griffiths is able "to direct emphasis in the historical past, . . . relegat[ing] the campaign for the vote to a heroic past and focus[ing] her characters' energies on struggling for economic independence and sexual self-understanding, issues resonant with today's audiences" (207).

Kelly's observation is certainly correct, yet Griffiths's program note for the 2007 premiere of the play at Alberta Theatre Projects in Calgary's EPCOR Centre for the Performing Arts begins by acknowledging the feminists of the first wave and earlier as her "philosophical ancestors" and ends by noting that "[j]ust outside the EPCOR Centre is a sculpture dedicated to these ancestors—we walked by it every day on our way to rehearsals. It's Nellie McClung and her gang, celebrating that, in 1929, women became legal 'persons'" ("Playwright's Note: *Age of Arousal*"). Beyond subverting the subversion of historical chronology that distinguishes her play, in which first-wave political activism is made to predate the present action of the plot set in 1885, Griffiths here brings *Age of Arousal* and its seemingly historical gender and sexual politics into the present moment by locating the play in relation to contemporary Calgary, where the feminist past is a notable feature of the downtown landscape. Barbara Paterson's bronze sculpture of the "Famous Five"—McClung, Emily Murphy, Henrietta Muir Edwards, Louise McKinney, and Irene Parlby, who together fought for women's right to be recognized as "persons" eligible to serve in the Canadian Senate—is prominently situated across from the EPCOR Centre for the Performing Arts (now Arts Commons) and alongside Olympic Plaza on 8th Avenue, installed in 1999 to commemorate the seventieth anniversary of the women's legal victory.

As Kelly and Shelley Scott ("Sickness" 41–42, 52) both note, the critical context for Griffiths's adaptation of *The Odd Women* was third-wave feminism's increased sensitivity to diversity and complex intersectional identities across gender, sexuality, class, and race. Thus, whereas Gissing's characters are all oriented, whether successfully or not, toward heterosexual relationships—even Mary, whom Gissing represents as having at one time been in love with her much younger cousin Everard and as initially being angry at and jealous of Rhoda's developing relationship with him because of her own lingering romantic feelings (236)—Griffiths represents a broader spectrum of sexual and gender identities. This spectrum ranges from Mary's lesbianism; to Rhoda's bisexuality; to Monica's polyamorous desires encompassing Everard and other male lovers but also, seemingly, Mary (*"Flirting, can't stop flirting, my body does it all by itself"*); to Virginia's cross-dressing; to Alice's celibacy or asexuality (*"the sex act is not a necessity for everyone, not a necessity for me"*) (*Age of Arousal* 45, 100; italics in original).

In *Sexual Anarchy* (1990), the title of which is borrowed from Gissing's statement about his era, Elaine Showalter links nineteenth-century debates about odd women to comparable media-fuelled debates a century later about the toll exacted by second-wave feminism on women's personal happiness and how women influenced by feminist advances risked becoming modern odd women, so to speak, by delaying marriage to establish their careers and in doing so compromising their ability to find husbands and experience motherhood (35–36; see also Scott, "Sickness" 53). This conservative "backlash" against the gains of second-wave feminism, documented by Susan Faludi in her 1991 bestselling book of that title, anticipated yet also differed from the neoliberal phenomenon of post-feminism that arose in the 1990s alongside the emergence of third-wave feminism. As defined by Angela McRobbie, post-feminism is "an active process by which feminist gains of the 1970s and 1980s come to be undermined," with popular culture in particular being "perniciously effective in regard to this undoing of feminism, while simultaneously appearing to be engaging in a well-informed and even well-intended response to feminism" (255). McRobbie's key example of post-feminist popular culture is *Bridget Jones's Diary*, initially a newspaper column by Helen

Fielding that traced the romantic trials of a thirtysomething singleton (odd woman) and later a bestselling novel (1996) in the chick-lit genre as well as a popular film adaptation (2001), both of which were followed by sequels. As McRobbie explains in her account of the operations of post-feminism, through "tropes of freedom and choice" ascribed to "the category of 'young women,' feminism is decisively aged and made to seem redundant." In this way, she argues, "post-feminism positively draws on and invokes feminism as that which can be taken into account, to suggest that equality is achieved, in order to install a whole repertoire of new meanings which emphasise that it is no longer needed, it is a spent force" (255).

At the end of her essay on her research for *Age of Arousal*, Griffiths admits to having sometimes felt ambivalent about being labelled a feminist. She acknowledges, however, that through her occasional small betrayals of feminism, she "cheated [her] own sense of self" ("A Flagrantly Weird Age" 166). There is something uncomfortable in Griffiths's choice in *Age of Arousal* to represent Mary and Rhoda as lovers only to have Rhoda find Mary to be not quite enough in the face of Everard's masculine sex appeal ("Playwright's Note" 19; *Age of Arousal* 103), of which she becomes aware in the course of Griffiths's invented scene of his gynecological examination of Mary, and then to have Mary tacitly threaten to exercise her class privilege and economic power over Rhoda in order to hold on to her as a lover, thus killing Rhoda's desire for her entirely. Nevertheless, *Age of Arousal* represents an important affirmation of feminist commitments and concerns, particularly against the context of post-feminism in popular culture from the 1990s through to the present (Gill).

Like Lucas Hnath in his recent play *A Doll's House, Part 2* (2017), Griffiths ironizes the idealism of Gissing's nineteenth-century proto-feminists and her own twenty-first-century transformation of them into first-wave feminists by having them envision their goals as achievable in the comparatively near future.[5] In the final speech of *Age of Arousal*, Rhoda says first to Virginia

---

5   In Hnath's sequel to Ibsen's *A Doll's House*, Nora returns to her husband Torvald's house fifteen years after walking out on him because she needs to obtain the divorce that she mistakenly assumed he had arranged in the immediate aftermath of her departure. At the end of the play, she observes that in the years since she left her marriage the world

and Alice, "The fire has been lit, it is burning through society with fero-
cious speed, no household is safe, the world is moving," and then to Monica's
baby daughter, now named after her mother, "In thirty years, it will all be
accomplished" (133). This closing line—seemingly so different from Gissing's
original ending—has sometimes been played for laughs, yet it might also be
seen to have an air of wistfulness and melancholy,[6] pointing toward a future
moment for the characters (circa 1915) that is almost a century before the
future occupied by the audiences of Griffiths's play in 2007—a future in which
the extent of the attainment of the goals of her historical characters remained
an open question. On the one hand, then, the play's ending suggests an alternative model for raising children, with Virginia now "*dashingly dressed in
men's clothing*" and the school that she and Alice dream of opening in Gissing's
novel presciently envisioned as "Day Time Care" (*Age of Arousal* 128, 130;
italics in original). On the other hand, were she to live to be one hundred
years old, the orphaned baby girl to whom Rhoda's forward-thinking final
line is addressed would die in 1985, in the midst of feminism's second wave.

Griffiths herself died in September 2014, a month before the sexual-
assault scandal relating to Toronto-based CBC radio host Jian Ghomeshi

---

has not changed as much as she expected it would in terms of the attainment of freedom,
but that it will someday and that she hopes she will live to see it. Married for eight years
and the mother of three children in Ibsen's original 1879 play, this older Nora, returning
home circa 1894 and performed in the Broadway premiere by sixty-one-year-old actress
Laurie Metcalf, would of course have been long dead by the time Hnath scripted her for-
ward-looking parting words in his 2017 play.

6   Jerry Wasserman's observation that Rhoda's closing line is one of *Age of Arousal*'s
"biggest laugh lines in production" ("Linda" 390) is confirmed by Kevin Prokosh's review
of a 2009 production by Theatre Projects Manitoba, in which he states that "Griffiths has
the last laugh with the parting joke about the inevitability of gender equality in the early
20th century." Similarly, Adrian Chamberlain's preview of a 2017 production by Theatre
Inconnu in Victoria, British Columbia, quotes director Wendy Merk as stating that the play
"concludes on a cheekily ironic note, in which a character predicts all feminist battles soon
will be won." *Calgary Herald* critic Bob Clark's comment that *Age of Arousal* "poignantly
broadens to embrace the future" suggests that the original production at Alberta Theatre
Projects captured the more ambivalent tenor of Griffiths's ending.

broke on the cusp of a wave of sexual abuse and misconduct scandals in the film and media industries, as well as in the heart of Toronto's theatre community.[7] The so-called "#MeToo" Twitter campaign—an example of the use of social media for feminist activism that has been seen by some as indicative of feminism's fourth wave[8]—has made patently clear that neither the sexual liberation nor the professional and financial autonomy of which Griffiths's nineteenth-century characters dream has yet been fully attained.[9] The ending of *Age of Arousal* might thus be understood less as a joke than as the essence of the play's "fabulism," to return to Griffiths's previously cited term—a moment of "utopia in performance" in Jill Dolan's sense: that is, of utopia not as something already arrived at but, rather, as "always in process, always only partially grasped, as it disappears before us around the corners of narrative and social experience" (6). *Age of Arousal*'s "fabulous" ending, gestically crystallizing the "fable" that is at play in the play, is thus an instance of "fleeting [intimation] of a better world" (Dolan 2) that is utopic not only for Rhoda and for Monica's baby in the context of the late nineteenth century but also for Griffiths's own contemporary and future audiences.

---

7   In early 2018 Albert Schultz stepped down as artistic director of Toronto's Soulpepper Theatre in response to accusations of sexual assault and harassment alleged by four actresses to have occurred between 2000 and 2013. The Jian Ghomeshi story broke in the *Toronto Star* (Donovan and Brown) shortly after Ghomeshi himself announced on Facebook that he had been fired by the CBC for his involvement in rough sexual practices that he claimed were consensual. Criminal charges were laid against Ghomeshi relating to a number of incidents with different women that were alleged to have taken place between 2002 and 2008. Although acquitted of those charges at his trial in 2016, Ghomeshi later signed a peace bond and formally apologized to a separate complainant, Kathryn Borel, for sexually inappropriate behaviour at work at the CBC between 2007 and 2010.

8   For a brief summary of the debate about whether social media activism constitutes a fourth feminist wave, see Gill 613.

9   The #MeToo movement on Twitter arose in October 2017 in relation to the exposure of widespread sexual abuse of women over several decades by Hollywood movie producer Harvey Weinstein, which in turn gave rise to a wave of similar accusations against numerous other men.

Dolan writes that "[p]erformance's simultaneity, its present-tenseness, uniquely suits it to probing the possibilities of utopia as a hopeful process that continually writes a different, better future" (13). Kelly's description of the feminist history play genre suggests a similarly utopic dimension in women playwrights' use of feminist historiography in theatrical restagings of women's and feminist history:

> The feminist history play embodies a contradiction: it has emerged from a critical . . . response to oppression within and exclusion from the national story, but it is also skeptical of the completeness and truth of any historical narrative, including its own. Thus the feminist history play offers itself as a provisional, sometimes ironical, and often open-ended commentary on the desire to know the past, to inherit a past, and the likelihood that such knowledge and inheritance is imperfect. (211–12)

As noted previously, Hutcheon has pointed out that "stories adapt just as they are adapted" (31), while Sanders has observed that adaptations "frequently . . . adapt other adaptations" and that adaptation is a kind of "incremental literature" (13, 12). A processual and provisional utopian performative emerges through Griffiths's poignantly ironic pointing toward a more perfect feminist future at the end of her restaging of feminist history in her early twenty-first-century adaptation of Gissing's nineteenth-century novel. In turn, that performative foregrounds the processual and utopian nature of adaptation as it evolves stories to new critical contexts through the dual gesture of replication and transformation. This ironic looking forward from the end of *Age of Arousal* may in turn establish grounds for further adaptations of Gissing/Griffiths in relation to as-yet-unknown future ages of feminist arousal.

THE TRAGIC MAGIC SHOW OF *ALIEN CREATURE: A VISITATION FROM GWENDOLYN MacEWEN*

BRENT WOOD

On the eve of the new millennium Linda Griffiths charmed audiences in Theatre Passe Muraille's dark, intimate Backspace with a solo performance as poet Gwendolyn MacEwen delivering a final revelatory monologue before her death. *Alien Creature* invoked MacEwen's noble and tormented spirit at a downtown Toronto intersection in which the crux of the drama itself, a dialectical struggle between the magical and the tragic, was uncannily manifest. Queen Street had formerly hosted vaudeville theatres where the young MacEwen was entranced by magicians and escape artists, and farther west still loomed the Queen Street Mental Health Centre, which had housed her disturbed and abusive mother. Walking north from Theatre Passe Muraille through the residential neighbourhoods east of Bathurst, one might pass the Robert Street house in whose basement apartment MacEwen, one of the "magic women, alien creatures" haunting the social scenes of Toronto in the 1960s and '70s, drew her last breath in a fatal effort at detoxification (*Alien Creature* 14). A prodigy who aimed to expand her horizons beyond the here and now, MacEwen ironically found her professional and personal worlds shrinking as she aged—a process symbolized on stage by the spotlight's broad pool of white slowly closing in to a pinpoint. Griffiths rendered MacEwen's story as a tragedy in which faith in magic fails to halt the heroine's downfall yet offers a hint of redemption in a flicker of ghostly light. *Alien Creature* captivated audience members through the internal tensions of this tragic magic show in which the poet, a magician "without quick wrists," ultimately loses faith in her own illusions and hits the limits of her escape-act tricks (30, 45).

In developing the play, Griffiths approached her subject much the way MacEwen's friend Margaret Atwood approached the private feelings of nineteenth-century Ontario pioneer-gentlewoman Susanna Moodie when she crafted her book of poems *The Journals of Susanna Moodie*—reading between the lines of published texts and interpolating what might have been left unsaid. Unlike Atwood, however, Griffiths also incorporated many direct quotations from her subject's works, suitably recontextualized. The resonance of the script with MacEwen's final collection, *Afterworlds* (1987), and her precocious early work provides a sense of depth to Griffiths's portrayal while facilitating ironic observations on the poet's inner world. Because she was playing MacEwen at the end of her life, Griffiths drew often from *Afterworlds*, whose poems develop themes of time travel, transcendence of death, primacy of experience over poetry, and expansion of self beyond the ego. Just as *Afterworlds* completed the "visionary circle" begun with MacEwen's early work, Griffiths included allusions to poems from *The Rising Fire* (1963) to show how the poet's end lay in her beginning. The play also makes key conceptual and stylistic references to poems from MacEwen's collections *A Breakfast for Barbarians* (1966), *The Shadow-Maker* (1969), and *The Fire-Eaters* (1976), and, when dramatizing her obsession with a male muse, alludes to her ambitious but unsuccessful novel *King of Egypt, King of Dreams* (1971). Griffiths also borrowed lines and scenarios from Rosemary Sullivan's biography *Shadow Maker: The Life of Gwendolyn MacEwen* (1995) and Brenda Longfellow's subsequent documentary film *Shadowmaker: The Life and Times of Gwendolyn MacEwen* (1998).

Griffiths's creative ability to evoke a convincing private persona by reading between MacEwen's published lines and public gestures derived from the identity the performer felt with her subject. When she took centre stage alongside a magic trunk at Theatre Passe Muraille, Griffiths was forty-six years old, the same age MacEwen had been when she died precisely a dozen years before. MacEwen was already trapped in a downward spiral of poverty, alcohol, and loneliness when Griffiths first gained notoriety with her solo show *Maggie and Pierre* in 1980, but Sullivan's biography kindled a posthumous interest in her work. A previous account of a self-dramatizing Canadian-born writer, *By Heart: Elizabeth Smart, a Life*, had earned the University of Toronto professor a nomination for a Governor General's Literary Award. MacEwen proved a more captivating and sympathetic subject as the tragic qualities of her life came into focus, and this time Sullivan won the prize. The biography inspired Longfellow's documentary, for which Griffiths provided the voice of MacEwen and some narration. Griffiths had chanced upon MacEwen's work at a vulnerable moment in her own career, discovering a fellow independent female artist struggling to succeed artistically and financially in a business-dominated culture. Griffiths told herself, "Don't do a show about Gwendolyn MacEwen—this is so obvious"—then, while recording for the film, felt that she was "coming into" the poet. Griffiths said she truly felt she could "channel" MacEwen at the time she embarked on improvisation sessions toward developing *Alien Creature*, a process central to her theatrical practice (McLeod 96). Griffiths described the script as emerging from a spontaneous imaginative union of the two artists, exploring questions around the cost of art, such as, "What do you have to give up, or should you give up? and how much pain related to how much gain?"[1] Griffiths pointed to the "belief that poetry was coming back" as integral to the work. In that belief resides the play's hope, centred on the image of the artist descending to the underworld in the mode of an epic hero. Nevertheless, following the lead of Sullivan's biography, *Alien Creature* subsumes the poet's heroism within a tragic framework. Its final ironic moment occurs with the death of the poet as a result of desperately trying to *avoid* drinking the alcohol to which she had become addicted in the course of a life devoted to mythopoeic acrobatics without a safety net.

Layering her own creative process over her subject's, Griffiths rehabilitated MacEwen's mythopoeic mission while making her story resonate with new overtones. One scenario in particular illustrates the affinity that drove Griffiths to mount *Alien Creature* in November of 1999. Addressing an audience gathered years later at the SOULO Theatre Festival in Toronto on the subject of her five solo shows as a writer-performer, Griffiths conjured the image of a

---

1   All quotations from Linda Griffiths come from her lecture at the 2014 SOULO Theatre Festival in Toronto, recorded and posted on YouTube. See "LINDA GRIFFITHS."

descent deep into the earth's interior to a cave with ancient paintings on its walls to describe how she had felt when developing and presenting those works. She referred to a Werner Herzog documentary on the Chauvet cave in the south of France, behind whose sparkling stalactites lurk paintings made 30,000 years ago. The film, *Cave of Forgotten Dreams*, premiered in 2010 at the Toronto International Film Festival, but the figuration of psychohistorical creativity as a frightening trip deep into a cave with grotesque animals waiting at the bottom was a trope already familiar to Griffiths, one she had used in *Alien Creature* to portray the solo poetic process of Gwendolyn MacEwen in the form of a Wonder Woman–like adventure tale. Explaining her metaphorical conception of the creative process behind the solo shows, Griffiths said, "Thinking of things as ancient always helps me to do them . . . Maybe I don't live in this time. Maybe I live in some other time." MacEwen often expressed a similar sentiment and sought to experience reality in the mythic terms of deep time. Fascinated by the ancient languages and cultures of the Mediterranean world, MacEwen concentrated her energies on imaginatively responding to the interface of timeless forces and symbols with contemporary experience, including her own relationships. Griffiths has her character Gwendolyn acknowledge the danger of such a lifestyle: "You can start to live in ancient places so an electric light bulb looks indecent and cars rather cruel . . . There are days when I wander the streets as a stranger and an exile and all the electronic waves in the air become absolutely too much too handle" (37).[2] In truth, the descent into the underworld signifies a journey back through personal psychology as well as cultural evolution into primal areas of our own consciousness, where we encounter ancient archetypes linked to fundamental human experiences. One of MacEwen's frequently anthologized poems, "Dark Pines Under Water," portrays this descent in a Canadian landscape:

> But the dark pines of your mind dip deeper
> And you are sinking, sinking, sleeper

---

2   This essay follows Griffiths in referring to the protagonist of *Alien Creature* as "Gwendolyn," while using "MacEwen" to refer to the poet herself.

In an elementary world;

There is something down there and you want it told. (*Gwendolyn MacEwen, Volume One* 156)

The attitude expressed by MacEwen in this stanza, addressing herself as well as her readers, aptly illustrates Griffiths's own artistic determination to plumb the depths of the psyche.

Alien Creature establishes its tragic frame at the outset as Gwendolyn warns the audience that she will die in the end—though not from suicide, distinguishing herself from the poet Sylvia Plath, who took her own life just as MacEwen's star began to climb. The element of magic is also introduced here, along with the play's title, when Gwendolyn characterizes herself as one of "those magic women, alien creatures" who once thrived in Toronto (14). The stage tricks start with fire from Gwendolyn's fingers—"creative sparks"—as an old trunk springs open autonomously on a stage suddenly flooded by light, from which she extracts a bottle and a glass. Inviting the audience into her space, Gwendolyn slides easily from heroical rhetoric into simple rhyming couplets, a carnival-barker poet gifted with the innocence of a child. In fact, MacEwen seldom used such regular rhymes, and audience members familiar with her work may have sensed Griffiths drifting out of literary character (a possibility acknowledged in the notes to the published script (8)). However, the rhyming couplets provide an essential childlike quality to the middle-aged Gwendolyn, conveying a key dimension of the poet and providing a counterweight to the tragic decline. The couplets end abruptly when, via lighting changes and posture, Gwendolyn "gains twenty years in moments" and begins drinking (16). Midway through the play, Gwendolyn again slips into rhyming couplets concocted by Griffiths as she returns to the trunk to write a poem, but instead takes out manacles and asks an audience member to lock her up—not because she wants to escape, but because she wants to remain bound, unable to write. Yet her desire is thwarted as the manacles fall away, and she compares her ironic frustration to that of escape artist Harry Houdini, completing a quotation from the poem "The Magician" that she had begun after the first round of rhymes (30). Gwendolyn resumes rhyming for a moment shortly thereafter as she ponders madness and children, but this time without the pretense of creating magic. From this point onward the tragic gravity exerts its fateful force as Griffiths reveals the fatal flaw in Gwendolyn's character: the "fantastic loneliness" produced by the intense desire for a male counterpart to reflect the other half of her imagined self, forever thwarted by her inability to admit anyone to her innermost psychic circles.

After Gwendolyn's magical rhyming invitation collapses into a rant about the violence of commercialism and a lament for her idealistic, successful younger selves, she acknowledges the tragic irony of the metabolic acidosis that precipitated her death by throwing her body into seizures—"not from drinking but from stopping drinking. Stopping dead" (21). Her subsequent descent to the cave creates the most compelling scene in the play, launched unexpectedly from memories of comic books and horror movies. Gwendolyn comments on the boom-and-bust cycle of poetic inspiration and suggests that she's out of ideas, getting drunk alone reading Marvel comic books and waiting to watch a Jack Palance movie on TV at four a.m. Griffiths borrows the image of MacEwen eating two fried green peppers for dinner from a comment in the documentary made by publisher Barry Callaghan, then draws on biographical passages concerning the poet's fascination with American actor Jack Palance, a running joke between MacEwen and her friend Aviva Layton (Sullivan 370). In October 1986, Layton sent Palance's mailing address to MacEwen, who replied with a note comically exaggerating her schoolgirl nerves about the prospect of writing to him. A year later, just two weeks before she died, MacEwen reportedly phoned Palance in Hollywood, but didn't get to speak with him (381). Palance had been a leading man in 1950s Westerns, but also used his distinctive visage to great effect as a character actor, and this ability to play dark roles as well as romantic heroes made him attractive to MacEwen. Thinking of Palance, Gwendolyn indulges herself in a ranchland fantasy as she quotes from her poem "Blue" from *Afterworlds*: "Body of many wings, beloved, body of many blue wings" (*Alien Creature* 21). Palance may have come to MacEwen's attention in 1968 when he portrayed Dr. Jekyll and Mr. Hyde for a TV movie—a role that, as we will see, had great personal significance for her. Following his success as Mr. Hyde, Palance played Count

Dracula in a TV movie, and was used as the model for the title character in the Marvel comic book series *The Tomb of Dracula* (Field 99). Associating Palance with comic-book adventures, Gwendolyn finds that her fantasy triggers a memory of a Wonder Woman tale, which turns into the cave-descent scenario.

Griffiths likely discovered the Wonder Woman image in a discussion by Sullivan of the allure of comic-book heroines for the twelve-year-old MacEwen. Sullivan quotes at length from MacEwen's personal journals, from which the poet herself borrowed for her poem "Fragments from a Childhood" in *The Fire-Eaters*, where she imagines herself in the boots of Mary Marvel and Wonder Woman (39–41, 391). "The Marvel Family has no quarrel with God," wrote the young MacEwen; "neither does Wonder Woman, but then she's a pagan and makes her peace with Greek statues. Later you learn there is a distinction between Wonder Woman and Sappho, but not now. You don't like Wonder Woman because her uniform is American" (40). MacEwen pondered the philosophical limits of two-dimensional icons, reasserting her own powers of imagination and her willingness to encounter the sublime as more important than the comic-book heroine's mere power of flight. Griffiths follows suit by having Gwendolyn insult Wonder Woman's American-flag skirt, raises the stakes by characterizing the Amazon as "a suck and a slave" with a "bad hair-do" who "never sold many comics," and nods to the growing girl's emotional need for the heroine (22). In her chapter "A Room in Winnipeg," Sullivan reaches for clues regarding MacEwen's response to a bloody bathroom episode in which her mother sliced her own throat in a fit of madness. The nine-year-old MacEwen (known as Wendy) was forced upstairs by her older sister Carol in hopes of sparing her the full view, but the moment lodged in her consciousness as a primal scene of fear, abandonment, and chaos, which Griffiths uses the descent fantasy to dramatize.

Gwendolyn recounts a tale in which Wonder Woman is elected by the Amazons to "save the universe and all the gods" from the Eve of Destruction, "prophesized since the beginning of time" and about to be realized by "a Being, a titanic energy force of great evil" who is "chained deep beneath the island of the Amazons" (*Alien Creature* 22). Gwendolyn begins to act out the story as she recounts it in third person, physically assuming the role of Wonder Woman while maintaining the narrative. The heroine makes her way through spears, traps, flames, and eyes gleaming in the darkness on her way through the caves in search of the monstrous Being. She finds herself in a cage, which Gwendolyn realizes "is made of intellect, each bar a language, each bar an iron concept." The cage is "lowered to the very centre of the earth where no one has ever gone before" and she finds herself "in a nursery . . . sweet and pink." She opens the cage door to confront an abandoned beast-child, filthy, warped, and hairy, with talons and fangs (23). The beast-child is just as frightened as Wonder Woman, who reaches for it, drawn by pity, only to be overpowered in its clutches. The heroine desperately tries to retreat to her cage of intellect but is suddenly overcome with sleep. "Even as the creature and its poisons burrow deeper and deeper inside her" she hears a strange lullaby: "You're nothing but a nothing, you're not a thing at all" (24). As the beast-child strokes Wonder Woman's hair, Gwendolyn confesses, "I can't find a way for her to win." After a brief pause, Gwendolyn regains energy, exclaiming, "that's no way to sell comics!" and, contrary to her earlier comment, now proclaims that Wonder Woman *will* be saved by her physical strength after all. She throws off the creature, stabs it, and runs to the cage, thus delaying the Eve of Destruction for another millennium. The cage is drawn up to the earth's surface, and Wonder Woman emerges "bleeding and victorious," embraced by her mother and cheered by the Amazons—but "no one notices the shadow of the creature following behind her." A giant shadow is projected over the stage walls, toward which Gwendolyn steps, about to enter, before suddenly whirling around on the audience to rail against the utilitarian forces that prevent her from being able to pay her way through life with her imagination (24–25).

Griffiths manages to embody a range of psychological perspectives in this vignette, showing MacEwen as both the young artist-hero Wonder Woman and the monstrous beast-child abandoned to eternal loneliness, perceived as a source of danger and destruction. At the same time, the creature also symbolizes MacEwen's mother Elsie, pacifying her daughter while reinforcing her insignificance, then casting a shadow across her life. As a girl, Elsie survived her own primal moment of terror underground when German Zeppelins loomed over London during the First World War, which contributed to a growing bipolar disorder and the tortuous upbringing of her daughters. The large shadow suggests the lingering effects of childhood trauma and the ongoing torment endured by MacEwen from her mother as well as from her father, who was driven to drink and thence to poverty by his wife's psychosis. As Gwendolyn attempts to rebound through a fantasy about poetry's impending cultural cachet, the shadow of her parents falls over her, with Alick begging for money and Elsie deriding her as a cheap Queen Street hooker (27).

In 1966 MacEwen had written, "you have the Jekyll hand you have the Hyde hand" in her poem "The Left Hand and Hiroshima," which Gwendolyn quotes before embarking on her second rhyming sequence in an effort to write about her psychotic mother and alcoholic father (*Alien Creature* 27; *Volume One* 81). Griffiths invokes the Jekyll-and-Hyde-hand image to represent the extremes of optimism and pessimism, MacEwen's inheritance from her mother's psychology, between which Gwendolyn knows lies a "sacred little path" (27). "The Left Hand and Hiroshima" features the poet claiming responsibility for the bombing of Hiroshima in the Second World War, putting herself in the place of the warrior-pilot who destroys cities and traumatizes families like her own. MacEwen hints at the common figure of speech "the right hand doesn't know what the left is doing," blaming her "abominably strong" left hand and punning on "right" in a paradoxical assessment of her craft:

> only because my poems are lies do they earn the right
> to be true, like the lie of that left hand at night
> in the cockpit of a sad plane trailing God in its wake. (*Volume One* 81)

The lying-to-be-true paradox is a common conceit among writers, but in MacEwen's case the metaphor combines with the conception of poets as "magicians without quick wrists" to figure poetry as mere stagecraft, the literary equivalent of smoke and mirrors, creating illusions in hopes of enacting *real* magic in the audience's minds and hearts (*Alien Creature* 30). Likening the division of her self into the Jekyll-and-Hyde, civilian-and-warfaring elements, MacEwen implies that in order to cope with her reality, her professional side

must distance itself from the part dangerously in touch with primordial violence. MacEwen invites her audience to share the responsibility, to become
accomplices to the creation of Hell on earth in the form of atomic incinera-
tion with the line, "you have the Jekyll hand you have the Hyde hand, /
my people, and you are abominable" (*Volume One* 81).

Griffiths brings out this identification between MacEwen and her audience particularly strongly in *Alien Creature* when she borrows two parts of
the last sentence of "The Magician," a poem from *A Breakfast for Barbarians*
addressed to Raymond Lowe, a Canadian illusionist whom MacEwen may
have encountered as a child in Winnipeg. Following Gwendolyn's first rhyming spree, she says, "Finally, then, do all my poems become as crazy scarves, /
issuing from the fingers like a coloured mesh, / and you, magician . . . " (*Alien
Creature* 17; *Volume One* 89). Griffiths lets the quotation trail off suggestively
as if addressing the audience members as magicians, whereas the original
line carried on: "you, magician, stand as they fly around you." This burst of
MacEwen's real poetry after the rhyming sequence stops its magical parody
short, but Gwendolyn runs with the idea of the scarf as exotic accoutrement
and carries it too far with "shards of ancient pottery" and "bits of lapis lazuli,"
triggering the abrupt dismissal of her own romantic imagination as "bullshit"
(17). Her self-denigrating skepticism echoes a sentiment expressed in "The
Magician," in which MacEwen compares her poems to Lowe's stage tricks,
calling her art "more a lie anyway / than the lie of these illusions / secret-
ing realities in the twitching silks" (*Volume One* 88). The poem concludes
with MacEwen flinging poem-scarves around Lowe in a vain but beautiful
attempt to mimic his astonishing theatrics while he stands "silent as Houdini
who could escape from anything / except the prison of his own flesh" (*Alien
Creature* 30). Griffiths inserts this line in the midst of the next round of
rhymes, when the magic becomes an escape act and Gwendolyn sheds her
manacles too easily. On the next page she speaks in second person, putting the
audience and herself in the position of the escape artist "wrapped in an old-
fashioned straightjacket" inside a coffin submerged in a water boiler inside a
tank. "You've done this trick a thousand times, but this time you can't get out,"
Gwendolyn tells us. "You're looking for some image that will set you free" (31).

The magic theme of *Alien Creature* was inspired by MacEwen's lifelong fascination with magicians, documented in Sullivan's biography and evident throughout the poet's work. Magicians and escape artists figured prominently in MacEwen's psyche, their stage acts inspiring her efforts to release herself from her impossible family trap. As a child she was treated to a show by magician Harry Blackstone in her own home, and as a young woman saw him perform at theatres on Queen Street. There she also encountered escape artist Mario Manzini, with whom she carried on a correspondence by mail (Sullivan 38, 68–70). Manzini wrote her from New York about his performances with the Ringling Bros. Circus, in which he freed himself from elaborate ropeties inside a water boiler sealed in a packing case and replicated the "Chain and Water Torture Cell" performed by Houdini (83). A letter (reprinted in the biography) prompted MacEwen's poem "Manzini: Escape Artist" in *A Breakfast for Barbarians*, and this same image in *Alien Creature*. At the age of eighteen MacEwen sought refuge from her alcoholic father and institutionalized mother in an esoteric world of imagination by writing her first novel, *Julian the Magician* (86). MacEwen wrote in the first person, assuming the voice of the wandering Julian who seduces audiences with his art but is dangerously seduced in return, caught up in "post-performance hysteria" (87). In a tragic turn Julian becomes a martyr, driven by his unconscious to imitate the life of Jesus, performing apparent miracles until he himself must be sacrificed. Later, living on Ward's Island after breaking up with poet Milton Acorn, MacEwen struck up a relationship with Bob Mallory, a painter who dressed like a magician in daily life and obsessed over the esoteric and the mystical, inspiring a number of poems in *The Rising Fire*. Sullivan observes that Mallory too became a tragic figure, outcast from society for his obsession with "our cosmic predicament" (151, 156).

In *Alien Creature* Griffiths uses literal and figurative images of darkness to evoke this same tragic strain in MacEwan's own life. Between invoking Houdini and picturing herself in a Manzini-like escape act, the lights that had been on the audience dim as Gwendolyn extemporizes on the motif "poets love the dark" with a string of allusions to her poetic history. In addition to the dark, she proposes, poets love "drunken clocks," a reference to

"The Drunken Clock," the title poem of MacEwen's early self-published collection, which contrasts two kinds of mechanical timekeeping: "Clocks count forward with craze, but / bells count backwards in sober grace" (*Volume One* 35). "Electric gardens" are next on the list, alluding to "Universe And: The Electric Garden" from *The Rising Fire*, which depicts the poet walking "warily" through a vibrating space in which "electrons like / mad bees / circle," a line Gwendolyn adapts in her offer of "electrons like mad bees circling your head" as a sample experience (*Alien Creature* 32). Griffiths subtly introduces the subject of MacEwen's lovers in the next items on the list, "kindled children" and "strange breakfasts," alluding to "The Kindled Children" and "Strange Breakfast" from *A Breakfast for Barbarians*. The poems are addressed to an unnamed but inspirational counterpart who kindles a fire to entertain children and shares metaphorical breakfasts which have "broken the past / hungers, hungers that were controlled" (*Volume One* 74). Following the third iteration of "poets love the dark," Gwendolyn describes her creative process beginning with an unwanted "realization" about the patterns in her life that make her sick, causing her to "sink right into [her] guts." She observes that "the poem may or may not be dark, but the moment is always dark" (Griffiths, *Alien Creature* 32). "I have a sense of humour. The dark doesn't," she remarks after a grotesque sexualized suicide image. "Take my dark. Please. Take my dark. A joke," Gwendolyn tells the audience, mocking herself by hinting at the old Henny Youngman stand-up comedy line "take my wife . . . please."

The darkness motif ends abruptly as Gwendolyn pivots to comment on love and sex. The stage is flooded with light as she quotes from "Marino Marini's Horses and Riders" from *Afterworlds*: "together for one second we are light." This line borrowed for the play is preceded by "Enter my darkness, I give you / My darkness" in MacEwen's poem about sexual passion in which lovers are figured as horse and rider who "collapse together in the catastrophe of love" (*Gwendolyn MacEwen, Volume Two* 142). Gwendolyn proceeds to display her reluctance to let go of her second husband Nikos Tsingos (a musician from Greece), comments on her un-hip sense of sex as a "sacrament," expresses her hopes that she was a "good lover," reveals her self-consciousness about having many men, and exposes her need for them to help stave off the one she knows will be her last, "Lord Death," addressed in "The Tao of Physics" and "The Grand Dance" in *Afterworlds* (*Alien Creature* 35; *Volume Two* 95, 144). The interweaving of sex, death, and art is made explicit as Gwendolyn quotes from "You Can Study it if You Want" from the same volume: "Poetry . . . / is the sound you make when you come and / why you live and how you bleed / and the sound you make or don't make when you die" (Griffiths, *Alien Creature* 36). Inspired by this epiphany, she asserts that poetry is "coming back" now at the "Eve of Destruction." She pulls two tongues of flame from the walls of her apartment, then quotes from "Second-Degree Burns" from *The Fire-Eaters*: "We all have second-degree burns / And they hurt but the hurt doesn't matter / The living flame of the world is what matters" (36). Gwendolyn begins to speak of herself in third person, sliding into the story of the ancient Egyptian king Akhenaton and his sister-lover, protagonists of her novel *King of Egypt, King of Dreams*, their sexual exchange figured as flames that keep her from her "fantastic loneliness" (38). Gwendolyn remains in the desert but travels forward thousands of years in an allusion to *The T.E. Lawrence Poems* (1982), in which MacEwen cleverly assumed the voice of Lawrence of Arabia, the apex of her efforts to meld male and female, east and west, poet and adventurer (Wood, "No-Man's Land" 142). Finally Gwendolyn comes around to acknowledging her first husband, Milton Acorn, the much older poet and "stinky man" MacEwen married when still a teen. "He sent his scent after me to the day I died," laments Gwendolyn, pivoting again toward the final phase of the play in which her tragic decline is recapitulated.

After portraying her subject's career in terms of a circle steadily shrinking around her, Griffiths painfully links MacEwen's psychological torment with her art. Gwendolyn reveals a deep sense of shame through her slurred words, raves in the voices of her mother and father, and quotes from two poems about terror and poetry. The first is "The Red Bird You Wait For," the poem that opens her 1969 collection *The Shadow-Maker*:

It is moving above me, it is burning my heart out,
I have felt it crash through my flesh,
I have spoken to it in a foreign tongue,
I have stroked its neck in the night like a wish. (*Alien Creature* 46;
Volume One 151)

MacEwen's red bird appears as an avatar of the sublime experience behind poetic inspiration, not a humanoid male muse this time, but a velvet cape that morphs into the wings of a bird with claws "gloved in fire." Gwendolyn repeats, "don't touch me!" then quotes from a poem called "But" from *Afterworlds*: "Beware! I now know a language so beautiful and lethal / my mouth bleeds when I speak it" (*Alien Creature* 46). Here the "breathless Poem" is figured as an eternal entity "out there in the large dark and long night," speaking to MacEwen and saying, "Do not hate me / Because I peeled the veil from your eyes and tore your world / To shreds, and brought / The darkness down upon your head. Here is a book of tongues. / Take it" (*Volume Two* 104). Finally even the well of terror runs dry as Gwendolyn laments, "then there are no poems there is no fire there is no breath there's a weight and a shadow. There is nothing because you are nothing," then slips back into the "you're nothing but a nothing" lullaby the beast-child sang to Wonder Woman in the pit of the earth (*Alien Creature* 46).

At this point MacEwen's muse becomes a Grim Reaper character offering Gwendolyn a way out. "The trap gives way under your feet the basement is at the very centre of the earth but you think there's an escape there's got to be," she exclaims, whereupon a man with cold eyes, Beatle boots, and long hair begins knocking on the door. Gwendolyn remarks on having rejected his late-night overtures in the past, but this time invites him in. Yet when he offers a special drink, she rebuffs him, choosing to live in spite of the pain. "I knew his lips would taste like sand," says Gwendolyn, pouring sand from the glass she's been holding as she walks her visitor to the door. The magic trunk opens again on its own, and, despite her rejection of death by intoxication, Gwendolyn signals her demise by telling the audience, "I'm sorry, but I did warn you" (49). The tragic framework is reinforced as she repeats a short speech from the opening of the play, telling the audience that she was both a brave fighter and a coward.

An ending for a visitation from Gwendolyn MacEwen more appropriate and powerful than the one conceived by Griffiths can hardly be imagined. Having brought the play's tragic tension to its ironic, inevitable resolution, Griffiths leaves the final words to the poet herself, discoursing not on the illusions of art, but on its loving core and its potential to supersede the bounds of time. The play concludes with a pair of quotations from *Afterworlds*, first from "The Lion" and then from "Past and Future Ghosts," carefully chosen to redeem painful mortality with the perspective of the infinite:

> I swear by all the famous, ancient lions I have known
> That all the mighty children yet to come
> will foster finer stars,
>
> For they are the true lords, born of morning,
> whose coming will call us down like a deck of cards.
>
> . . .
>
> I am starting to haunt you. I am starting right now. (50)

Dedicated to California poet Robert Duncan, a prominent literary figure in the 1960s who died two months after MacEwen, "The Lion" affirms the magical power of love. "To love is to be remarkable, and flawless," she writes, to achieve immortality, to "wear the yellow crowns / Of all the gods" (*Volume Two* 141). "Past and Future Ghosts" treats the overcoming of time in a different way, as MacEwen posits that ghosts may haunt us from the future as well as the past. "We all just move from room to room in these time-houses and catch glimpses of one another in passing," she writes. "As a child in this one house I used to see this older woman who was myself grown up, and thirty years later I went back there and met the child, who was waiting for me to come . . . Look out—you who inhabit the rooms of my future—I'm coming after you. I'm starting to haunt you, I'm starting right now" (129). This last line chilled audiences at Theatre Passe Muraille as the stage went dark, confirming Linda Griffiths's faith in herself as a medium for the spirit of her artistic predecessor.[3]

---

3   Three years after Griffiths died, Beatriz Pizano played the role of Gwendolyn in a production of *Alien Creature* featuring lighting and set design by Trevor Schwellnus, technician for the original performance. Pizano brought the spirit of Griffiths back to Theatre Passe Muraille along with that of MacEwen, the three performers together affirming the power of art to transcend time and mortality in the play's final eerie pledge.

THE ENIGMA OF TRUTH IN
THE DARLING FAMILY

ANN WILSON

Linda Griffiths's *The Darling Family* (1991) is a two-hander that dramatizes the discussions between two characters, identified as "SHE" and "HE," as they decide whether or not to terminate an unplanned pregnancy. Subtitled *A Duet for Three*, the play depicts the couple's conversations, as well as the private thoughts of each of the characters, about the impact of the pregnancy on their lives. The play is spare, performed over ninety minutes, "*without intermission, set, sound, or lighting cues*" (9). There is an intimacy to *The Darling Family*, not just because of the private nature of the decision the couple is making, but because this is theatre pared down to its most basic element: actors before an audience. Shelley Scott notes that *The Darling Family* charts the "progression of a relationship between the two characters" that engages members of the audience who are aware that they are watching a play "in an unusually unmediated, intimate experience" ("Bodies" 202). While this intimacy gives a feeling of being "truthful," the references to J.M. Barrie's *Peter Pan* serve as subtle, but consistent, reminders that a play is artifice, a medium that is characterized by pretending. *The Darling Family* is a fruitful site for considering how truth is constituted in the theatre. Rather than a character speaking the "truth" or actors finding the "truth" of their character, Griffiths's play suggests that "truth" in the theatre is primarily constituted in two interrelated ways: the trust between actors that allows the action to seem real, and the audience believing in the veracity of the action unfolding on the stage.

In an interview with Judith Rudakoff, Linda Griffiths said, "For me, the spiritual element of theatre is the most important part" (18). She explains that she draws on a range of spiritual traditions, including those of First Nations people and on New Age philosophies (19). This perspective is evident in *The Darling Family*, which opens with a stage that "*is completely bare except for a dish containing sage and matches, and two rock crystals on the floor. The two actors enter. SHE lights the sage and smudges herself with the smoke. HE smudges himself. SHE fans the smoke towards the audience, then blots the sage*" (11). Both the sage and the rock crystals are associated with purification, the former in rituals of First Nations' people, and the latter by adherents of New Age philosophies. The actors playing SHE and HE cleanse themselves, and then the audience, through the smoke that symbolically forges the relationship between the actors, and between them and the audience. This ritual of cleansing immediately implies that the theatre is a space that has a sacred element. In the course of *The Darling Family*, the two characters grapple with their feelings about SHE being pregnant, often taking the risk of being candid and vulnerable with each other even though their relationship is relatively new. The audience watches the actors purify themselves and then seamlessly become SHE and HE, blurring the distinction between actors and characters, thereby allowing the possibility that the purification of the actors extends to the characters.

We quickly learn that neither SHE nor HE has dealt with a pregnancy before. They have been together for only three months, during which time HE was away for two weeks (20). HE comments, "We don't really know anything about the other person" (22). As a result, they navigate a highly charged decision—either to terminate the pregnancy or to have some sort of sustained connection with each other through the child—by being cautious with each other. When HE is probed by SHE about his feelings, he responds that he is concerned (23), a sentiment he reiterates when SHE asks him twice more how he feels (25, 34). His expression of concern is innocuous, compatible with the indications that he sees the pregnancy as SHE's responsibility, not his. In anger, HE initially blames her, saying, "Well the next time you're moved to put the cap in sideways, I wish you would let me know," suggesting that SHE should take responsibility for her mistake, as if he is not implicated (24). Later, when lying in bed with SHE, HE relents, thinking to himself, "It's not fair that she has to go through this" (26). He tries to empathize. HE tells SHE, "I understand fully the difficulty of the choice, as fully as I can being a man" (33). Still later in the play, HE says of himself, "I'm not a bastard, I'm not going to run. They're talking about me, all those women friends of hers. About how I don't want it. About what a bastard I am. How can you be a man and not a bastard? I am not a bastard. I am not a bastard" (37).

There is no point where HE seems genuinely accepting that this is a problem that SHE and HE face as a couple because, from his perspective, they are not in a committed relationship that is ready for a child—a third in the duet. HE tells SHE, "Raising a child is about good timing for two people, a man and a woman" (32). From HE's perspective, the decision about the pregnancy is SHE's. HE is intent on protecting his sense of himself as a decent man who will support her. That said, the fact that HE mentions that he is not going to run suggests that the antithesis—running away—is on the horizon of possibility. He thinks to himself, "*She looks at the moon and thinks of the child, I look at the moon and think of escape*" (35). Finally, he admits to himself, "*I know what I want. I can't do what I want. Run run run / run to the farthest corner of the globe fly away and come back in twenty years*" (50).

His response to the pregnancy may arise from a self-acknowledged lack of maturity. HE comments, "When I look in the mirror, I see a boy's face" (45). Earlier, HE tells SHE, "I always thought that I was Peter Pan" (33). The subtitle of *Peter Pan* is *The Boy Who Wouldn't Grow Up*, suggesting that HE is chronologically a man, but emotionally he is a boy. He does not have the option of an escape to the world of Neverland, which, as SHE indicates, is where boys go "to become pirates and never go home" (33).

HE: But they do go home.

SHE: Ah yeah, all except Peter Pan.

HE: I always thought I was Peter Pan. (33)

There are other references associating HE with Peter Pan. Later, HE says to himself, "*I hate the thought of touching, don't want to touch anything*" (51).

Here, Griffiths echoes Peter's aversion to any sort of physical expression of affection, expressed in scenes like the following from J.M. Barrie's play:

WENDY. Peter!

(She leaps out of bed to put her arms round him, but he draws back; he does not know why, but he knows he must draw back.)

PETER. You mustn't touch me.

WENDY. Why?

PETER. No one must ever touch me.

WENDY. Why?

PETER. I don't know.

(He is never touched by anyone in the play.) (98)

Like Peter Pan, *The Darling Family*'s HE is not keen on accepting the responsibilities of being an adult and accepting the consequences of his actions.

On the other hand, nor is SHE. When HE tells SHE, "I always thought I was Peter Pan," her response is, "I always thought I was Peter Pan" (33). As HE expresses an aversion, unexplained, to being touched, SHE expresses a similar aversion, expressed in relation to the physicality of sexual intimacy: "I don't know why I fucked anyone" (50). Her reasons for being wary of sex are clear. She has been participating in therapeutic sessions with someone named Peter, in which he takes her "into this . . . past life or something" (42). SHE recovers a memory of being a twelve-year-old girl who becomes pregnant as the result of being raped by her father, recounted in the monologue that opens the play. This memory shapes her response to the pregnancy. SHE wants to escape: "Get on a plane a boat, a train a bus, never tell anyone where you are, run away with your secret that soon won't be a secret when will this adolescence end I don't want to fly out the nursery window, yes I do I still do, no big belly / just me I'm flying so far so high" (51).

The status of the recovered memory is unclear. The fact that the therapist's name is Peter allows for the possibility that he is taking SHE to a form of Neverland—a place she has never been—as she explores past lives, a practice that is associated with "New Age" spirituality. In *The Darling Family*, SHE's memory of being raped by her father is described as looking

> like a European movie, all muted colours, things that don't look like anything at first, and then it's as if the camera pulls back and the focus clears. There's a white crumbling room with bodies sleeping in dirty clothes, and it stinks. I know that I'm in a ghetto of some kind, that there are hundreds of rooms like this, stacked and twisted, crushed together. Crying babies, shouts, swearing, bells tolling, cross-eyed children, no one knows what year it is. (11)

The hallucinatory quality of the memory makes it seem unreal. At the very least, the memory is incomplete. SHE says that after he raped her, she may have killed her father, a grotesque figure with "a bloated face, big bulging brown eyes with lots of veins, all watery, like a dog's" (11). She says, "I don't know. I can't remember" (12). This memory—real or false—affects SHE's response to her current pregnancy.

Griffiths titled her play *The Darling Family*, suggesting that as much as HE and SHE identify with Peter Pan, they may also have a lot in common with members of the Darling family. For example, he recognizes that he would like to have a child at some point in his life, but not now (32). He says, "I think a child needs to be cared for. I know this may sound corny but I think of it like the Darling family in *Peter Pan*, you know, the Walt Disney version? That Victorian house with the nursery? . . . The nursery is all set up for those kids, it's a play just for them, they're wanted and they know it" (33). This sentimental memory of the animated adaptation does not correspond to its source text, the play by J.M. Barrie, one of whose earliest stage directions reads, "The

Darlings could not afford to have a nurse, they could not afford indeed to have children" (88). Barrie makes other allusions to the Darlings' financial strife, including remarking that Mr. Darling "is very conscientious, and in the days when MRS. DARLING gave up keeping the house books correctly and drew pictures instead (which he called her guesses), he did all the totting up for her, holding her hand while he calculated whether they could have Wendy or not, and coming down on the right side" (90).

In Barrie's play, the issue is less whether the Darlings wanted children and more whether they could afford to raise children. It is unclear whether, at the time Mrs. Darling stops doing the books, she is pregnant with Wendy and whether her anxiety results from a realization that she and her husband will struggle to raise a child because money is tight. Initially, before the action of the play, Mr. Darling seems to be able to handle the strain of having children when financial means are modest, as suggested by his willingness to relieve Mrs. Darling of the responsibility of reviewing the finances to see if they could afford to have a child. By the opening of Barrie's play, George Darling is a petty, insecure man who feels that his respect within the household is undercut by Nana, the family's dog, who has been engaged to care for the Darlings' three children, Wendy, Michael, and John. Mr. Darling says of Nana, "I refuse to allow that dog to lord it in my nursery for one hour longer" (96). His sense of masculine authority being eroded is occasioned, the play suggests, by his status in a workplace where he has no discernable identity: *In the city where he sits on a stool all day, as fixed as a postage stamp, he is so like all the others on stools that you recognise him not by his face but by his stool, but at home the way to gratify him is to say that he has a distinct personality*" (90). Similarly, the characters in *The Darling Family* have no proper names that publicly individuate them. They are named generically as "SHE" and "HE," suggesting that Griffiths does not want the audience to receive the story as being that of two individuals but, rather, she seems to want the audience to understand that the experience of addressing an unanticipated pregnancy is one that many couples face.

In *The Darling Family*, as in *Peter Pan*, financial considerations factor into the decision about having a child. HE offers half of everything he earns to support the child if SHE decides to have the baby (43). The offer seems generous, but the reality is that HE's capacity to earn a stable living is tenuous, given that he is a musician. SHE responds, "Money isn't a question" (42), to which he insists that it is (43). HE's perspective, acknowledging that there are financial costs involved with having a child, is the more realistic of the two. By insisting that "money isn't a question," SHE shows a naive—even a childlike—response to the responsibilities of parenthood, including the financial costs.

Peter Pan playfully, but forcefully, suggests that parents can indeed be childish. In the opening scene of the play, Wendy and John pretend to be their parents:

WENDY. Now let us pretend we have a baby.

JOHN *(good-naturedly)*. I am happy to inform you, Mrs. Darling, that you are now a mother.

WENDY *(gives way to ecstasy)*. You have missed the chief thing; you haven't asked, "boy or girl?"

JOHN *(crushingly)*. That is just the difference between gentlemen and ladies. Now you tell me.

WENDY. I am happy to acquaint you, Mr. Darling, you are now a father.

JOHN. Boy or girl? (90)

Parenthood, in *Peter Pan*, is represented as being a performance, a point made clear when Mr. Darling returns from work to find his children play-acting the family with Wendy as the mother and John as the father. In order to get Michael to take his medicine, Mr. Darling is cajoled by Wendy to take his own medicine, thereby becoming a role model for his younger son. Instead of taking the medicine, Mr. Darling behaves as if he were a petulant child, saying, "There is more in my glass than in Michael's spoon. It isn't fair. I swear though it were my last breath, it is not fair" (94). While in *The Darling Family* there is not the same pronounced sense of an adult being childlike as there is in *Peter Pan*, there is a clear sense that neither SHE nor HE is ready to assume the considerable responsibilities, both emotional and financial, of raising a child. SHE says, "I may act like I don't really have a hold on things. But I have got money in my RSP account, and I do keep it together in the regular world" (44). That self-assessment by SHE of her maturity and emotional readiness to raise a child is at odds with her earlier comment that

> Everything will be better if I have a doll baby, a baby doll. The baby
> will take everything, everything everything never have to think again
> if you have a baby doll. Never be alone again. It'll always want some,
> you always have to give something, it always has to take something,
> when you have a baby doll. (41)

While children play with dolls and pretend to be parents, babies are not dolls. They are not toys. They are human beings who require a lot of care. When SHE characterizes the baby as a doll, she casts the baby as inanimate, as an object that will fulfill a void within herself. Later, petitioning a deity—"goddess, god, spirits, trees, all the books I've read. God. God of my childhood"—SHE suggests that having a child will "heal" her (52). HE describes SHE as someone who needs eleven hours of sleep, who takes two hours to get of bed, who "can't go to sleep at night without the light on, who eats Valium like candy, with inexplicable pains, insomnias, flus that don't go away for months . . . " (47).[1] HE describes a woman whose neurotic behaviour is reminiscent of a child: SHE can't sleep without a light on, Valium is like candy for her, and she gets aches and pains without an etiology much like children feign illness to avoid activities in which they don't want to engage. This childlike woman wants to play at being a mother, referring to a live baby as a "doll."

---

1   The latter is a somewhat odd comment given that HE and SHE have only known each other for a few months.

Peter Pan begins with John and Wendy pretending to be their parents. Wendy, the eldest child, is the author/director of the role-playing: "Now let us pretend we have a baby" (90). She continues to direct the action when she and her brothers accompany Peter to Neverland, where they meet the lost boys who invite Wendy to be their mother. She feigns that she cannot assume the role because she "is only a little girl" who has "no real experience" as a mother (116). The boys reply, "That doesn't matter. What we need is a nice motherly person" (116). Replies Wendy, "Oh dear, I feel that is just exactly what I am" (116). In Neverland, she presides over her brood of "lost boys," ensuring that they keep the rules about "hands-off-the-table" and "no-two-to-speak-at-once" (126–27). She has cast Peter in the role of the father to the children, a role for which he has little aptitude. John comments that Peter Pan is not their father, "He did not even know how to be a father until I showed him" (127).

Similarly, in *The Darling Family*, HE was four years old when he first met his biological father, who he recalls could not look at his son but chose instead to play cards with the friends who had brought him to the meeting. As quickly as HE's father arrived, he left (57). HE, like Peter Pan, does not know how to be a father. Just as Wendy scripts Peter, SHE scripts HE, a point that is not clear until the end of the play when he realizes that SHE made an appointment to have an abortion as soon as she learned that she was pregnant (54). Reasonably, HE asks, "Then what the fuck have you been putting us through this for?" (54). Initially, SHE doesn't answer HE's question, but finally admits that she wanted "contact" (55).

HE: You made your decision the minute you heard, didn't you?

SHE: It wasn't like that. Yes, I thought I should make the appointment right away but I really thought that we might be cancelling that appointment, I didn't know, I still don't know . . .

HE: Say it, just say it.

SHE: Yes I knew. Not the first minute, but the minute after. You're right. I'm a liar, somewhere I am a liar. (55)

His response suggests that HE feels as if he has been manipulated by SHE; given that SHE did not disclose that she had made the appointment for the abortion, HE is correct. SHE was partially candid from the outset about her motives for wanting to talk: "I want this to mean something, be a way for us to talk, I want to know what you are feeling . . . I want to know all the contradictions, the feelings, I want to tell you mine. This will either break us apart or make us closer than we ever would have been" (27). SHE is using conversation as a way of forging intimacy. SHE is engaging HE in a dialogue that SHE believes will constitute them as a couple through the performative act of speaking as if they are a couple that is close and loving. Mimicking intimate speech is not the same as having true intimacy, a point made clear in *Peter Pan* by Wendy, who naively believes that if she addresses Peter as if he were the father of the lost boys, he will become their father. Acts of speech are powerful, but the act of speaking is not enough to create an emotional connection between two people. There is a distinction between actual intimacy and the performance of intimacy.

Shelley Scott, one of the few academics who has published on *The Darling Family*, suggests that "everything has been designed to focus on the actors": a choice that powerfully engages the audience ("Bodies" 202). Scott continues by discussing the film adaptation of *The Darling Family*, which was produced in 1994, roughly three years after the premiere of the stage version. The screenplay was adapted by Griffiths from her script for the stage; the production featured Griffiths as SHE and Alan Williams as HE. Scott suggests that "the film medium offers the spectator too much distraction—the two characters' apartments are shown, a musical soundtrack is introduced, camera tricks are explored—thus dissipating the unrelenting focus on the actors" ("Bodies" 202). Scott also suggests that "in the case of *The Darling Family* the film medium throws the emphasis onto content, when the unique form of this piece should have enhanced the spectator's involvement with the experience, as in the original theatre production" ("Bodies" 202). Scott's point is that for a viewer, watching the film does not replicate the experience of seeing the production, a point of which Griffiths seemed aware. She commented to Henry Mietkiewicz, "Making *The Darling Family* into a film is something I've wanted to do for a long time, because I was always convinced it would acquire a special sort of life on screen. I also liked the idea that the piece would be preserved and go on living in that form." The film was a mnemonic to remind its audience of the play, but not intended to record the play as a theatrical event. It is an adaptation of the play that through the addition of a host of elements—for example, locations and a soundscapes—gestures to the source text (the stage play of *The Darling Family*) but creates a new work, even if retaining the characters and their situation.

In the article by Mietkiewicz, Griffiths told the reporter, "The characters in [*The Darling Family*] are very faulty, terribly infuriating people. But I like to think they finally attain a kind of nobility by reaching a rare, hard-won point of honesty." In what way, though, do they reach that "point of honesty"? The minimalism of the playscript means that there is no way to assess if what the characters are saying is truthful. The audience cannot gauge if HE or SHE is telling the truth because there is no context: the relationship is too new for either to challenge the other; there are no other characters who respond to SHE and HE. The relationship exists within a self-contained, stripped down world on stage. The world of *The Darling Family* is its two characters, for neither of whom reality is limited to what is manifest. Through various aspects of New Age spirituality, they gain consciousness of aspects of reality that are not easily accessed, including the possibility of recollecting lives previously lived. For both SHE and HE, reality includes that which is beyond consciousness and, by extension, beyond language. SHE uses crystals, "to see with" and "to clear the mind," to bring the subconscious to the surface (40). SHE speaks of "other . . . realms . . . other frequencies playing on your life . . . " (29). HE says, "Our subconscious may be magical, that makes sense to me" (42). Within the fictional world of *The Darling Family*, reality and, by extension, truth are labile. Binaries—for example, reality and fantasy; truth and lies—are unstable, which challenges the audience who is invested in making sense of what it sees unfolding on stage. For *The Darling Family* to be a successful theatrical experience, the audience must believe in the conversations between the two characters as the expression of their private thoughts. It must believe not in the veracity of everything they say, but in the emotional veracity of the fledgling relationship that is marked by manipulation, role-playing, and the presentation of a recovered memory of a past life as an actual part of the characters' histories. The audience must be caught up in the exchange between the two characters and believe that what each is saying is true, even if only in the moment. The triumph of *The Darling Family* may lie in Griffiths's suggesting that the "truth" in relationships is not singular, but changing and contingent on the moment.

Griffiths characterized *The Darling Family* as a duet, a musical form that requires the two performers to listen to each other with care. The opening stage direction reads: "*HE and SHE almost never fight, they are almost never mean, they are almost never snide, they try to give each other the best side, they are polite, they are well read, they know things about things, they almost never fight, they almost never love*" (9). The two characters do listen to each other, even if as tentative performers. Given the minimalism of the play, the two actors performing *The Darling Family* must be skilled at performing the duet: adept listeners who harmonize occasionally, who take solo lines and form the interplay between them, contingent on listening and responding, and present a work of art.

The ending of *The Darling Family* echoes its beginning:

(SHE smudges herself. HE smudges himself. SHE waves the smoke toward the audience.)

SHE: Tell me that you love me.

HE: I love you.

SHE: I love you.

(SHE blots out the sage.)

Are we grown up now?

(Blackout.) (62)

The final line refers to the subtitle of *Peter Pan*: *The Boy Who Wouldn't Grow Up*. The question SHE asks is, has the process of talking taken them from their own version of Neverland in which each is Peter Pan, and allowed them to grow into a loving couple? Despite the declarations of love, with HE's being a response to SHE's request that he proclaim his love (another moment of her scripting him), there is no way of ascertaining the sincerity of their professions: are they true expressions of their feelings? HE has been "scripted" by SHE to participate in conversations in which the expectation is that he will express his feelings, exposing his secrets whether or not he so wishes. In the face of what amounts to manipulation, can HE fall in love with SHE? (49). Who is "we" of this couple? The characters of SHE and HE? Or is "they" Linda Griffiths, who wrote the play and performed the role of SHE in the first production in the Backspace of Theatre Passe Muraille, and Alan Williams, who played HE in the original production? The smudging that occurred at the beginning of the play took place in a liminal space. Who was smudging? Linda Griffiths and Alan Williams as actors? Or the characters of HE and SHE? It is reasonable to suppose that the final smudging marks the end of the play and the professions of love are not those of the characters, but of the actors expressing their closeness to each other. There is no way of knowing with certainty: truth in *The Darling Family* is an enigma. In theatre, which Linda Griffiths believed to be sacred, truth is what the audience believes to be true.

WALLIS: PORTRAITS OF "THAT WOMAN" BY TIMOTHY FINDLEY AND LINDA GRIFFITHS

SHERRILL GRACE

One day in December of 1936, a six-year-old Timothy Findley watched in surprise as his mother opened the newspaper and cried out, "My God! The King is going to marry Mrs. Simpson" (Findley, "The King" 32). This cry confused him because the only Mrs. Simpson he knew was the family's cleaning lady, "a woman so dour and endlessly unhappy" that he could not understand why "the King would want to marry her" (32). Young Tiff Findley, a Canadian boy living in Rosedale, who already knew that his elders revered the royals, was not the only person to be incredulous at this news. Most of the United Kingdom and the dominions were vehemently opposed to the idea. Wallis Simpson (1896–1986), a twice-divorced American commoner from Baltimore, was stealing their king; she was generally known in England as "that woman," and in government and royal family circles the epithets were more disparaging.

Since December 1936, when the news hit the papers, soon to be followed by Edward VIII's abdication and then his marriage to Wallis in June 1937, a great many biographers, historians, novelists, playwrights, and filmmakers have wondered why he did it. What was it about Wallis that she could so beguile Edward that he would renounce the throne, bring upon himself scorn and rejection by his family, and consign himself to lifelong exile from his native land? Who was Wallis Warfield Spencer Simpson, and what did she hope to gain from marrying her king? By all accounts she was neither beautiful nor especially intelligent, but she was ambitious, witty, and charming—especially when it came to men. Even a biographer like Ralph Martin, who creates a flattering portrait of her, allows that she knew how to impress men by making them feel important, handsome, and virile. Martin knew Wallis, had interviewed her several times, and concluded that "for a petite woman" she exuded "a feeling of presence and size": "you always come back to her large, luminous, violet-blue eyes, piercing and intense. When she talked to you, it was only you she was interested in, and she made you know it" (9).[1] It seems that it was her capacity to make "you"—if you were a man—feel you were the centre of the universe that explained, in large part, her magnetism.

The backstory for Wallis's life, however, is far more complex, controversial, and mysterious than intense blue eyes and a knack for flattery suggest, and it is, therefore, a fascinating subject for artists who want to create a fictional duchess. The two Canadian versions of "that woman" I will discuss here are by Timothy Findley and Linda Griffiths.[2] Wallis plays an important, if minor, role in Findley's novel *Famous Last Words* (1981), and she is the central character in Griffiths's play *The Duchess: AKA Wallis Simpson* (1998). The similarities between their portraits of Wallis are so striking that I believe Griffiths had read Findley's novel, as well as some of the same sources he consulted. Despite the similarities, however, there are some key differences in these portraits, most importantly in the ethical dimensions of the texts and the character-ization of Wallis. Although both works engage with the theatrical concept

---

1   Martin's *The Woman He Loved* was one of several sources Findley consulted in his extensive research for *Famous Last Words*. Martin, an American, is biased in favour of Wallis and critical of the royal family, including Edward; he dismisses the notion that Wallis was seriously approving of Hitler or Nazi ideology, blaming that aspect of the Windsor story on Edward, and he argues that Wallis loved her third husband and had no desire to be queen. He also covers many of the bases that other historians and biographers explore in greater detail, including the possibility of a plot to install the Windsors on a puppet English throne after the Nazis had won the war. See also Bloch, *Operation Willi*; Maltby; Morton; Phillips; Sebba; and Urbach.

2   The number of historical romances, plays, television dramas, and films about the Windsors, or touching upon their lives, is large, and some of these are sensational. In his novel *Fatherland* (1992), Robert Harris depicts Edward as a restored king with Wallis as his queen in a pro-Nazi English puppet government. Among the actors who have portrayed Wallis are Faye Dunaway, Jane Seymour, Gillian Anderson, and Lia Williams.

of performance, in the novel this concept is necessarily a metaphor through which we read about Wallis behaving *as if* she were acting in a play, whereas, in the play, the performance is an embodied illusion created by Griffiths, a highly skilled actress who, in some ways, physically resembled Wallis.[3]

Famous Last Words is the fictional autobiography of Hugh Selwyn Mauberley, an American writer, protege of Ezra Pound, fascist sympathizer, and close friend of Wallis Simpson.[4] By telling his confessional story, which he writes on the walls of an abandoned luxury hotel in the Swiss Alps before he is assassinated in May 1945, Mauberley remembers his past life and his relationship with Wallis; in a sense he is her biographer, describing her appearance, her conversation, key events in her life, and the roles she plays in the history leading up to and during the Second World War. To him she is a consummate actor, always on stage, always in perfect makeup and period dresses by Elsa Schiaparelli, and always performing for an audience. Findley began his career as an actor and also wrote plays, so it is hardly surprising that one of the governing metaphors of this novel is theatrical performance. Another crucial metaphor—actually the key narrative strategy of the text—is memory: Mauberley is remembering his life and Wallis's, in the context of the years between 1924, when he first met her, and 1945, when he is killed.

If Griffiths knew this novel, then its theatricality and staging of autobiographical memory would have appealed to her. *The Duchess* is fundamentally a memory play, framed by an estate auction of Wallis's jewels, in which the auctioneer/stage manager, Noël Coward, accidentally conjures up the duchess herself, who arrives in a "*crash of thunder [as] a mad old woman*" (109)

---

3   This generic distinction, while fascinating, is a complex theoretical issue, which is further complicated by questions of gender performance and representation that extend beyond Wallis to include several other characters in both the novel and the play. Such a discussion is beyond the scope and purpose of this essay. Let me just add, however, that Griffiths's resemblance to Wallis Simpson—her own intense blue eyes and slender figure—contributed to her convincing and galvanizing creation of the character.

4   All references are to the 1982 paperback edition. Findley borrowed his Mauberley character from Pound's *Hugh Selwyn Mauberley*; for a detailed study of Pound's influence on the novel, see Scobie.

to recall and re-enact events in her life with the help of a supporting cast of characters she calls "ghosties." "I'm Faerie Queene now," she announces. "It's time to remember [. . .] I command you to remember" (115). Griffiths, who played the duchess in the Theatre Passe Muraille premiere of the play, created a tour de force role for her Wallis, who is ruthless, calculating, aggressive, and quite prepared to side with the Nazis if it will help her achieve her goal of becoming a queen.[5]

To appreciate the way Wallis is portrayed by Findley and Griffiths, it helps to recall the historical context and controversy surrounding Edward and Wallis. Debate about the politics behind the Windsors and their relationship with Nazi Germany between 1936 and 1945 continues to this day as more hitherto classified information becomes available to historians, but the basic issue concerns the degree of the Windsors' sympathy with Hitler's National Socialist agenda and their awareness of—possibly their active co-operation with—a secret cabal hoping to reinstall the duke as king with Wallis as queen after Hitler won the war. There is no doubt that the duke was pro-German; his ancestry was German, he spoke the language fluently, and he saw Hitler as a bulwark against the kind of communist revolution that had already taken the lives of some of his European cousins. He gave pro-German speeches, ostensibly to promote peace by reaching agreement with Germany, which embarrassed his family and infuriated his government, and in a widely covered 1937 tour he and the duchess visited Germany and met with Hitler and his top officials; Edward was photographed giving the Nazi salute. Wallis's political views are less clear. She was not well informed about world affairs and seemingly not interested in history, the British constitution, or the complexities of ideological conflict. Nevertheless, she appreciated the Germans,

---

5   Linda Griffiths certainly read about the Windsors and uses many factual details, but she did not, to my knowledge, identify her research sources. She did comment that she drooled over books about Wallis's jewels, and that she wanted to think "big"; see her interview in *CTR* 97. My warmest thanks to Cynthia Zimmerman for helping me appreciate this play. She interviewed Griffiths on 5 April 1998, has shared her findings with me, and has written the best discussion, to date, of this play; see "Introducing Wallis." My references are to the 2013 edition of the play.

who greeted her on the tour as Her Royal Highness, the title denied her by the British, and she wanted formal recognition, power, wealth, and prestige. Personal ambition was her motivation, status was her goal, and men were her ticket to advancement. She believed Edward had power, if she could make him use it effectively, and she saw that Hitler had power.

Rumours circulated from as early as 1939–1940 that a plot involving the duke and duchess had been formed by clandestine interests in England, working with officials in Hitler's inner circle, and that the chief conspirator in England was Joachim von Ribbentrop.[6] Since that time, enough information has surfaced to confirm the existence of this cabal, who was involved, and the details of its plans. The first major study to blow the whistle was Michael Bloch's *Operation Willi: The Nazi Plot to Kidnap the Duke of Windsor*, which appeared in 1984, three years after the North American publication of *Famous Last Words*. Several recent studies further confirm Bloch's findings and provide more information.[7] Clive Maltby's 2009 television documentary, *Britain's Nazi King?*, has certainly reached the widest general audience, and in it Maltby makes a strong case for Edward's pro-Nazi, pro-Hitler views, Wallis's close ties with von Ribbentrop, and the couples' awareness of the cabal and its plans for a "Dictator King" (Morton 59). The picture that emerges from the studies I have read is of a duke who was selfish, spoiled, and a playboy favourite with the public (until he abdicated), and of a duchess who was hell-bent on escaping the genteel poverty of her childhood, bettering her position in life, and ingratiating herself with wealthy people who could introduce her into high society. He was insecure and vain, fearful of his domineering father, King George V, and his judgmental mother, Queen Mary; she was strong-willed, calculating, and shrewd. Neither of them seems to have given

---

6   I have no evidence that Findley or Griffiths knew this but, at the risk of drawing attention away from the subject of Wallis, I cannot resist noting that von Ribbentrop (1893–1946) spent the years of 1910–1914 in Canada and claimed to love the country. He also loved parties, tennis, and the theatre, and in May 1914 he performed a love scene in a play in Ottawa. The moment war was declared, however, he vanished from the Canadian scene to return to Germany. See Bloch, *Ribbentrop*, and Lawson.

7   See note 1.

much thought to the impact of the war on Britain or the appalling atrocities committed by the Nazis. He spent the war years obsessed with winning her a title and preserving his wealth (neither of them paid taxes in any country); she devoted herself to clothes, jewellery, elaborate parties, and propping up a weak man with her ambitious strength. From 1940 to 1945 he was sent by Winston Churchill to Bermuda to be governor of the Bahamas, a minor post he resented in a place she viewed as an exile.

Summarized like this, the story of a charming prince and the woman he loved sounds sordid, which brings me back to my initial question: why would artists like Findley and Griffiths be attracted to these people and what, especially, did they see in Wallis? The Wallis presented by Mauberley in *Famous Last Words* is impressive for her style, ambition, and courage. She is seen by Mauberley as a survivor, intent on making it to the top despite obstacles. We also see around this Wallis, however, because Mauberley is a fascist who supports the cabal and wants to assist Wallis in her plans to become a queen. His view of Edward is jaundiced; he sees the duke as weak, vain, and ineffectual, in short as a man Wallis must support but does not love. Mauberley's Wallis makes her job the work of maintaining her ex-king, and she is coldly motivated by self-interest and the instinct to survive. He stresses the historical facts that she dresses well, entertains lavishly, and is witty, but he does not present her as interested in the war, except insofar as it has an impact on her life, or in political realities. Mauberley's own moral failings are worse than hers because, as an artist and intellectual, he should have known better than to support fascism; he was aware of the political scene in Europe and yet, like Pound, his mentor, he joined the devil's party.

In *The Duchess*, we see Wallis Simpson from different perspectives that complicate our picture of her. Wallis is initially conjured up by her friend Noël Coward and she appears to him as a deranged, withered old woman. But when she takes command of the play, she is instantly young, lively, attractive, hugely ambitious, and strong-willed. This Wallis seems capable of love for her three husbands and for a former lover, but she always has her own goals in mind. Inevitably for a memoir, she remembers herself in a good light, which holds true even in her sensational scene with Hitler, whose ideology does not worry her. Designer clothes, expensive jewels, luxurious homes and parties, and the pursuit of power and prestige are her consuming interests. Otherwise, she wants to dance, play popular American music, and have "fun." At the end of the play, we are left with a rather sad picture of an old woman who tried to reach the top, as she saw it, through men, each of whom failed her, and yet she tells Coward, and us, that after all she loved the duke. As Cynthia Zimmerman puts it, "[S]he is both a product of her times and a challenge to her times. Her drive to achieve, to have, is fierce. [She] is no soft woman accustomed to surrender. Rather, she uses her sexuality and her cunning to realize her own vaulting ambition" (iii).

Although both the novel and the play are primarily set in the period leading up to and during the Second World War, their emphasis on history differs, as does their focus on individual players in that history and their focalization on the historical drama. *Famous Last Words* is a richly complex historical novel with an inner fictional autobiographical story, and on both levels it explores some of the worst events of the twentieth century and the betrayals, personal and political, committed by people (real and fictional) who should have known better and acted ethically. Mauberley's story is framed by the two men who discover his corpse and his writing on the hotel walls: one is Freyberg, a captain with the American army that had liberated Dachau and was pushing the Germans out of Italy and through Austria; the other is his lieutenant, Quinn, who identifies Mauberley as a famous novelist and the man the Americans would like to arrest on charges of treason. Freyberg condemns Mauberley and refuses to accept his confession as honest; he cannot forget what he saw in Dachau and he wants the guilty punished and remembered as criminals. Quinn, however, is something of an intellectual who admires artists; he accepts what Mauberley writes as a sincere apology for his fascist beliefs and betrayals of country, truth, personal honour, and ethical responsibility, as an artist, to resist evil. For Quinn, the art exonerates the man; for Freyberg, the man and his art cannot be separated and the failure of the man debases the art. Mauberley, in Freyberg's eyes, is a self-serving hypocrite in a world all too eager to forgive and forget. In this novel, Findley presents revelations of the truth about evil, collusion, violence, and the lust for power, and he urges his readers to weigh the evidence he puts before them and, above all, to remember the past. The twentieth century to which he—through Mauberley, Freyberg, and Quinn—bears witness is a horror story for which we are all to some degree responsible.

The Duchess is, in Griffiths's words, a *"Canadian commedia dell'arte"* (101) with a society chorus; actors who play the role of Wallis's jewels; and comic scenes, verging on caricature and slapstick, juxtaposed with serious scenes meant to reveal human emotions and historical details. In her introduction to the 2013 edition, Sarah Rodgers claims that Griffiths "succeeds in human-izing a woman who had been demonized by an entire nation" (99). Unlike the novel, however, the play does not interrogate the wider political or ethi-cal issues or provide characters who explore, debate, and perform opposing views on historical events. Instead, one woman is the focus and Wallis is given some infamous last words: "There isn't a wealthy dinner table in the world that doesn't contain at least one true Fascist" (223). It's a great line, which may well ring true, but it does not question that reality. Wallis's memory play within the play is staged as a "[f]airy tale romance" (Coward's description of the Windsors' story, 108) with Wallis as the self-styled "Fairie Queene" (115). "Once upon a time" (115), the chorus chants as we are transported back in time to a moment when the betrayals and horrors of the twentieth century merge with one celebrity's life story. "I am the 20th Century [. . .] brutal and greedy and fun," Wallis tells us (230).

Mauberley and Coward are essential to these two texts. The famous last words of the novel's title are what Mauberley writes on the hotel walls; he is a homosexual writer, an auto/biographer, a Wallis fan "dancing in the lime-light" (98), and a witness to his times. He tries to stay on the sidelines, looking on, observing people and events, and he always remembers Wallis as a star performer. Coward is also a homosexual writer, who observes society and hobnobs with the rich and famous; as a playwright he is the perfect person to evoke Wallis and provide the stage upon which she can perform. Our first sighting of Wallis in *Famous Last Words* takes place in 1924 in the lobby of a Shanghai hotel, as Mauberley watches her sitting, waiting for a lover. In his mind's eye, he remembers her shedding "[s]uch treasure in the air" (66) that

she is, for him, unforgettable.[8] He describes "the lacquered chair on which
she sat" (70), and he tells us that "her face was lacquered," that she "never lived
without the application of a mask," and that "her hair was a masterpiece of
illusion" (73). This is the narrative stage on which he and she will form their
bond, with him as her faithful helper, and their dialogue, which Mauberley
records, could easily be performed. Coward, by contrast, opens the play as
one who is in charge of the "auction of the century" (107); he quickly dismisses politics, referring the audience of prospective bidders to the seventeen
conflicting versions of the Windsors' flirtation with a Nazi cabal—seventeen for the number of roses (or carnations) von Ribbentrop is said to have
sent to Wallis—but he is also the one who reminds Wallis that she does not
love *his* country and that he suspects she has told British military secrets to
von Ribbentrop (163). In the play, Wallis's entrance is more disruptive and
spectacular than what Mauberley recalls; this Wallis is determined to seize
control of Coward's show and represent herself. He wants her to go away,
but she refuses: "I want them [the audience/the bidders] all to know you
can't just get rid of women like me. We stick" (111). Moreover, she dismisses
Coward's warning about the Hitler rumours: "Everyone's sick of Hitler," she
announces. Then Wallis takes us back to China in 1922, but this scene takes
place in a brothel, where she will learn the sexual arts of Fang Chung and be
abused by her first husband.

   Both works include scenes in bed, and each scene is sensational. In
Famous Last Words we watch Wallis lead the duke, who has sunk into the
depths of self-pitying despair, into their stateroom on the *Excalibur* (the
American ship that took them from Lisbon to their exile in the Bahamas).
The duke watches as Wallis removes all her clothing, except her slip, and lies
down beneath the sheets; the duke climbs in after her "as one who climbs
aboard a lifeboat" (243). Once they are settled, she pulls a photograph on
the bedside table closer to them and tells him that it is his turn. He then

---

8   The passage quoted is from the "Envoi" to Pound's *Hugh Selwyn Mauberley* (127),
but here, and elsewhere in the novel, there are strong echoes of Shakespeare's *Antony and
Cleopatra* and *Much Ado About Nothing*.

makes a further adjustment to the position of the photograph and sighs. "Is she watching?" Wallis asks. "Yes." "Can she see us both?" "Indeed." "Good," Wallis replies. "Then shall we?" "Yes" (243). The photograph is of Her Majesty Queen Mary, dressed in mourning, "And what is more, she could not close her eyes or turn away as her son and his wife began their ritual" (243). What takes place on the bed is not described, except as "their battle," but the point of this perverse performance is to flout royal disfavour and demonstrate Wallis's efforts to prod the duke to stand up to his mother, to behave like a man, to assert his claims. What I find especially striking is the way Findley sets the scene as a double act of voyeurism: we watch the couple prepare for their ritual before the unaverted eyes of the woman in the photograph. By comparison, the sex scene in *The Duchess* is an explicit tour de force in which Wallis straddles Edward and performs Fang Chung on him and then takes off her black gloves to beat him with them. Before he reaches his climax, she has him repeat, "I'm the King of England and I can do as I like" (151). Their pillow talk then turns to National Socialism, and Edward describes Hitler as "a great man." Wallis is impressed, especially by Edward's assurances that when he is king he will have the power to do what he wants. Shortly after this, she will echo Edward's words by calling Hitler "a great man," and the stage is set for her 1937 meeting with Hitler.

Findley does not have a scene in which Wallis and Hitler meet, but he does explore the aftermath of the actual meeting when he has Wallis, von Ribbentrop, and Mauberley attend a lavish reception and dinner held in the duke and duchess's honour in Madrid in June 1940. Here, Findley has followed the facts of the Windsors' movements after war broke out; they did flee France; go to Spain, where the duke had loyal aristocratic allies (some of whom were in on the plot to kidnap him for the Germans, if necessary); and then move on to Portugal, where they stayed in Ricardo Ribeiro do Espírito Santo Silva's seaside villa near Lisbon. What occurs at the dinner in Madrid, however, is largely imagined by Findley and presented to us through the memory of Mauberley. Hosted by Franco's brother-in-law, with illustrious guests like the Duke of Alba and Infante Alfonso, as well as the duke and

duchess von Ribbentrop, and Mauberley, the dinner becomes a stage set for
a spectacle. And Wallis is the spectacle:

> There she was: resplendent. Wallis descending in a gold glass cage.
> Her hair was elaborately piled as I had never seen it before and held
> in place with lethal pins, and her body was sheathed in cerulean silk
> over which she wore a Mandarin's robe embroidered with a flight of
> birds. Her cage, of course, was a lift embossed with gold [. . .] and
> it fell, like a flake of ice, without a sound. Her eyes, as she descended
> were triumphant. (179)

During the dinner, Mauberley is seated with Wallis and von Ribbentrop, and
it is here that von Ribbentrop gives the cabal the code name "Penelope," in
honour of Wallis, who Mauberley sees as like Odysseus's loyal wife waiting
for her king and husband. Wallis has grown, at least in Mauberley's eyes, to
mythic stature, and she basks in this fame and attention.

In *The Duchess*, Wallis does meet Hitler, but the stage is set for this encounter by von Ribbentrop, who tells Edward and Wallis that he knows they have
been treated "with contempt" by the royal family and assures them that he
knows "a place where you will still be regarded as the sovereign [. . .] a kingdom that understands the role of good blood" (201). Act 2, scene 7, called
"Wallis and the Devil," illustrates just how tempted Wallis and Edward are by
Hitler's plan to reinstate the duke as king, with Wallis as queen. As this scene
opens, Hitler is seen painting at an easel and humming. Enter the duchess. His
tempting offer to her, however, does not include Edward. He insists that, when
he conquers England, she will rule beside him "because you understand power"
(207). She demurs—"I don't understand" power. "Liar!" Hitler screeches: "You
don't belong with that delicate blond boy. You want me. Look into my eyes. You
are a Nazi." Almost seduced by his desire to be chosen and "to choose who's
chosen" (207), she lies on the floor and invites him to "take" her, so she can
"suck [his] vision" (208). But before Hitler can get his pants down, she wavers.
She senses that he is going to lose the war; it is his moustache that provides
the clue: "You're going to lose. You can tell because of the moustache. [. . .]

It's a failure of style" (209). Then Edward enters and gives the fascist salute, but when Hitler tells him that he wants Wallis, the duke refuses and Wallis tells him that it is time to go. Still the duke hesitates: "If we let go of our dance with Herr Hitler, we lose our last bit of leverage on the world stage" (210). They will leave, of course, not because Hitler is a Nazi, but because he is going to lose. So who is the worst Nazi sympathizer—Wallis or Edward? Griffiths leaves the answer hanging in the air of self-interest and the desire to stay on the winning side. And is Findley's Wallis more culpable than Griffiths's? When we compare this point in the play with the Madrid dinner scene in the novel, there is little to choose between them. Both portraits of the duchess are ethically damning. That we, like that photograph of Queen Mary, cannot avert our eyes, resist our fascination with celebrity and scandal, condemns us as well.

Is there anything redeeming about Wallis Simpson in these two versions of her life? Perhaps, if we place our bets on sheer guts and on love. In both works she is seen—by Mauberley, Coward (to a lesser degree), and by herself—as heroic in her efforts to bolster Edward's confidence and support his claim to the throne and her royal title. He appears in both works as a vain, spoiled, ineffectual man with tainted political views; in both she has a lot to manage in return for considerable opprobrium, as well as money, elegant homes, jewels, designer clothes, and parties. But did she love this man? In *Famous Last Words* she says no; in *The Duchess* she says yes. A few months before her wedding to the duke at Candé, the estate in France belonging to the fascist industrialist Charles Bedaux, Findley's Wallis tells Mauberley that she hates Edward. Mauberley realizes that he must tread carefully because, if she refuses to marry Edward at this late stage in the 1937 game of thrones, much will be lost. In their private conversation, she tells her old friend that the duke has failed to keep all his promises to her: "I was going to be Queen," she protests, and the promise was not kept. "I hate him," she says. "I do . . . I hate him" (144). And then, in her fury, she shouts, "*hate*" (144; emphasis in original). But Mauberley convinces her to go ahead with the marriage because "anyone could hold the stage who had power" and she must always "*[b]e visible*" (144; emphasis in original). It does not matter after all if she really loves her husband, as long as she can play the part, perform her role, and win in the end. A few years later, during the Bermuda exile, Wallis and Mauberley are once more able to speak privately while they are dancing, but this time the roles are reversed: he dislikes dancing and is nervous that the cabal's plans are crumbling, so she advises him to "[p]lay it up, Maubie. Act" (335). This Wallis has become her actor's mask; she and her role are one and the same. In *The Duchess*, however, Wallis asks Edward on his deathbed what he loved about her, and he answers, "Your . . . innocence" (229). When Edward dies, she is furious, claiming that everyone has tricked her, and yet, with almost her final words, she tells Coward, "I loved him" (230). The auction resumes, Wallis dances *"like an old puppet"* (230), and the lights fade. With these two brief statements about innocence and love, we are suddenly left with a glimpse of a more complex Wallis, a Wallis with some depth, and a woman who refuses to be a victim or succumb to a supporting role in her husband's life or accept her public image as merely a gaudy spectacle.

Without question the story of Wallis and her ex-king has legs. The aftermath of her life extends well beyond her death and her fictional recreations, and the same must be said for *Famous Last Words* and *The Duchess*. With time, Wallis has come to be forgiven, if never entirely embraced or included, by the royal family. Queen Elizabeth II actually invited her to London when Edward died and treated her with respect, and Findley's novel could not be published in the United Kingdom until after Wallis died because her French lawyer was quick to sue anyone daring to defame her client. When the novel did appear in 1987, it was slammed by reviewers for maligning England's "Beloved Duchess" (Adachi). Findley was devastated by this ugly hypocrisy from a people who had once vilified Wallis and who, in some circles, continued to see her as a Nazi sympathizer and a greedy opportunist. To no small extent, this negative reception of the novel damaged its post-publication influence, even though it was a Canadian bestseller. To the best of my knowledge, *The Duchess* has not yet been staged in England, but if it were I expect it would be received with some controversy, but also with considerable interest. Some perceptions have changed since Wallis died in 1986, not least with the public's general sympathy for women who marry into the royal family. When the play was produced by Vancouver's Ruby Slippers Theatre in 2015, reviews were positive and Diane Brown's Wallis received praise. According to Brown, who had worked on the play with Griffiths in 2009, the play exposes the sexism of the early twentieth century that persists into the twenty-first century insofar as women are still expected to be passive helpmeets quietly channelling their ambition and submerging their talents in the service of men.[9] If ambitious women aspire to power on their own behalf they are, as Hillary Clinton's fate demonstrated, suspected of corruption and damned in the press and by segments of the public (including women).

Whether guilty or not guilty of purely selfish motives and Nazi sympathies, whether condemned or forgiven, whether a "Beloved Duchess" who stood by her man or the epitome of a conniving bitch, Wallis Simpson is part of an ongoing story of love, hate, political party collusion and corruption, and gender politics. These two works, so powerful in their theatrical recreation of her life and times, continue to challenge and fascinate us, not because Wallis Simpson was especially admirable—she wasn't—but because of what she can be seen to represent and for the light her life story throws on a violent, destructive period in the twentieth century. It is, perhaps, unfair to compare Findley's masterpiece with a two-act play; the scale and scope of the novel extend far beyond what the play attempts. But I believe the comparison illustrates how the personal becomes political, how celebrity can seduce us, and that each one of us has a duty to pay attention to what is happening at home and on the world stage. I see a definite cautionary element in these two works. Mauberley tells us to be wary of the deception surrounding us—everything "*is true except the lies*" (59; emphasis in original)—he says, and Wallis warns us that there is a fascist at every wealthy dinner table. Both works also warn against believing in innocence, our own and that of others, and both show us that we must not forget the past. *Famous Last Words* gives us a more negative take on Wallis than does *The Duchess*, but then Mauberley, for all his adoration of his Penelope, is more dangerous and manipulative than Coward. In the last analysis, this novel and this play, when placed side by side, invite us to reflect on who we can believe and how much we can, or should, forgive. Like political corruption, repression of facts, greed, and the lust for power, Wallis continues to haunt the stage of history.

---

9   See Warner.

WHO IS SHE?
A SUBJECTIVE ASSEMBLAGE
ON LINDA G.

DANIEL MacIVOR

Unlike Linda, *Lianna* didn't age well. When it was released in 1983, the second film directed by maverick American filmmaker John Sayles, it was remarkable. The birth of an American independent movement. Slow and banal, yet high drama. There was something awkward about its greatness. People don't have the patience for *Lianna* anymore. Or perhaps it's that *we* haven't aged well. Though I doubt even John Sayles has the patience for *Lianna* anymore. But at the time it was riveting. It was thoroughly *modern*. And though it seemed determined to be political, there was a teasing, self-conscious sexuality at play that made it feel a little too personal to be coldly political. Of course now I'm just describing Linda.

In the film there is a scene where Linda as Lianna is alone in the kitchen. She is sitting at the table and after a few moments she gets up and goes to the refrigerator and opens it. She hangs off the door a moment, gazing into the fridge, searching for nothing. That scene—more a moment really—is so arresting because Linda appears so uncomfortable in it. So self-conscious. I ask myself why, and I imagine Sayles asking Linda to behave as if she were alone in the kitchen. And I imagine how odd that would seem to Linda. How bizarre those concepts to her. *Behave. Alone.*

***

In her play *Heaven Above, Heaven Below* Linda played a character called only SHE in a verbal pas de deux with a man called only HE. We all knew who he was of course. Or thought we knew. He was Alan; he was Layne. Was he

Clarke, the other Daniel? It was delicious. It was poetic vérité, taken into an imagined future. Pure invention, but rooted in something real. It was punk Cassavetes dreaming of Ginsberg. I'm foggy on how it started. I may have suggested she do a sequel to *The Darling Family* (while we were having broccoli soup in Kensington Market sitting on stools at the counter of that big salad place across from the cool little theatre space where we were rehearsing *The Last Dog of War*), or perhaps it was her idea alone. Linda, darling, who really cares? And gloriously it came to be. And then she got sick and there was the show to do . . . or maybe it was the show to do first and then she got sick . . . it was a foggy time. Regardless, the show came to mean so much. Her producing the show. Her doing the show. Her getting through the show. I never discussed this with Linda, but there was a sense for many of us that this was the last chance to see Linda, not only in this role but in any role. If Linda felt that way, I do not know.

I flew in from Halifax to see the play. It was the last show. It was in Linda's preferred theatre at Passe Muraille, the Backspace—*that gorgeous black hole, that magical box*—and beautiful Layne Coleman was HE, and brilliant Karen Hines had directed it, and Linda was SHE. This was all a much of much in the best possible way. I was staying at Christie and St. Clair and I left very early because I felt I should walk. I should *think*, I thought. It was December. A mild night. I drifted south down the hill, skirted Rosedale then zigzagged through the Annex, hitting all the best streets. I wandered along Bloor Street and stopped for some pho. I backtracked from the pho place and through U of T, continued past the theatre to Markham Street, past Linda's red house. Just to see it. I made my way back down through the park by the open-air rink. I lingered there for a cigarette. As I came out at the top of Ryerson Avenue and walked toward the theatre I wondered if I should maybe go backstage and say hi. I was early enough. There was no one around. How odd. *No one around.* Twenty minutes to showtime and no one here? I expected a crowd.

I spoke with the kindly box-office person—who acknowledged that a 7:30 start time had proven to be occasionally problematic, yet continued to apologetically express, several times, that we were already ten minutes in and "no latecomers" had been the direct wish of Linda. A voice in my head was yelling, "Go apeshit! Get into this show! You flew from f'ing Halifax! Go Fucking Apeshit!" But I did not succumb. For Linda, I did not. And for this kindly box-office person, I did not. "Allow this person," I thought, "to proudly and unapologetically honour this wish." My only response to being turned away was to pathetically say, "I stopped for pho." The kindly box-office person smiled and shrugged, relieved.

I sat in the lobby, waiting. I took the opportunity to *think*. Maybe this was a good thing. I was atoning for decades of chronic lateness. I was being granted an opportunity to practise grace. I had been given this quiet time. I was visiting with ghosts. But foremost, I was honouring Linda's wish. For whatever reason, I was a latecomer and latecomers were not to be admitted. There was something holy in honouring that, in giving that wish—the gravity of that sentiment—space. This was right. This was essential.

By the time I got backstage word had already travelled to Linda in her dressing room. She was disbelieving and agog. She seemed surprised that they had taken her instructions so to the letter. I assured her that all was fine. She refused to accept "fine" and demanded of me, "Why didn't you go fucking apeshit!?"

***

There appear in one's world people who become avatars for a city. In the world of my Toronto there are several, and Linda Griffiths is one. She is a bit of Rosedale and a lot of College and an early Queen of Queen West. She is part of that Toronto crowd from Montreal who ended up in theatres. She is Bar Italia, equally the old world first and the film world second. She is the Cameron House, where outside one night she fell off her shoes, breaking her shoulder, probably while looking up into the moonlight, waving at that other Queen. She is the park around the corner from the theatre, by the rink, that park with no name, where so many of us found refuge after a difficult opening or a bad review, seething and drunk and smoking cigarettes. She is Kensington Market, all of the Market, all of its shops and all of its cafés and all of its books. She is Comrags on Dundas. She is Markham Street and that house, that red house, that black trim. How solid it stood, and still stands. And she is probably most of all Theatre Passe Muraille. Because that is where they've put her name on a lane where drunkards and poets gather.

***

Though Linda and I shared an understanding of how to embody our own work, Linda's vision was more fluid than mine and her opinion of narrative was different. I saw narrative as a tool, for her it was barbaric. In work like *The Darling Family*; *The Duchess*; *Age of Arousal*; *Games*; and *Heaven Above, Heaven Below*, Linda deigns to narrative. And in each of these works there is something fractured in the narrative line. This is mostly expressed in the actions of the characters—the psychological trajectory doesn't lift off or land, there are sudden odd choices, firmly held positions easily shift. Having worked with Linda I would say the reason for this is that she wasn't interested in narrative. She felt its necessity, in order to be produced, to remain relevant, to be celebrated, to be employed—but for her, narrative was restrictive. Artificial. Linda was going for something else.

In *Alien Creature* Linda tells us a story about the poet Gwendolyn MacEwen going to a bank manager to get a loan. MacEwen was asked for collateral, *what did she have that was worth something*? Gwendolyn goes home and gets her poems, her books, and puts the stack on the bank manager's desk and asks, "What's this worth?" and the bank manager is forced to reply sadly, "Nothing." It was clear watching her in the role that Linda loved telling that story. It was hers. She loved the horror of it, the truth of it, the dark hilarity of it. This was her at her best, when she shared her work with us this way, when she taught us. In performance Linda's presence usurped any need for narrative. She was the narrative. Her awareness of our presence, and of her presence with us. Her awareness of being watched. Of not being in the room alone. Of the truth of the lie. No walls within walls. In this thinking, theatre becomes less about story and more about exchange, and, specifically, about the author's presence in that exchange. It seems to me a key to her work might be in understanding that the presence of the author's voice in these plays is required. These plays are only *naturalistic-seeming*. Typically in naturalism the author's voice is expected to be hidden in story or character. For Linda these aren't stories about characters, they are actions about expressions, told in her voice. With her bemusement and her wonder and her outrage and her dark vanity and her deep heart.

***

The book launch of *Jessica* was an event in Toronto when it happened. I was living in the city then, but my work was focused more in the fringy queer scene. The launch was at Passe Muraille and the scene there had always been the cool kids in the drama class. No, in fact, these were the kids who didn't go to drama class at all; they went to art school; they went to Europe. Passe Muraille was the place where they removed the second floor so the lighting designer could get better positions for instruments. This was the place where their production of *Hamlet* was not simply *Hamlet* but the *Passe Muraille Hamlet*. Linda was Ophelia and Layne was her Prince. The whole gang went to Jamaica together and Linda wrote a notorious play about it. They were always doing something notable at Passe Muraille. *Jessica* was Maria Campbell's story. Linda and Maria had written it together. I didn't know much about Maria, but I knew she was a powerful woman. A Métis activist. In the premiere production in Saskatoon Linda had played Jessica. It was another time, but still a foolish idea, though innocent. Linda felt Maria's story was too important not to tell. At the book launch in Toronto wounds of that appropriation were still fresh. There was a very public dressing down of Linda, in front of an audience. She felt it deeply and wore it without protest. She, a settler from the land of Pierre Elliott Trudeau himself, the daughter of an airman trying to present herself as a sister of the moon. Linda was shaken. *Jessica* was not a subject Linda spoke of often but her mortification, her shame, was still heard in her voice decades later when she did. You could hear that she understood what it meant to be a Canadian, to be a patriot, the cost to others, the lie to ourselves.

***

Linda invited me to her house for tea and to ask a favour. This was 2007. We had become work friends. I wanted her to be in my play. She was always up for scheming. We were going to maybe make a thing together but we were having trouble finding a director willing to commit to dealing with both of us at the same time. I had first met Linda in the '80s when I was just out of theatre school and my journalist roommate was working on *Theatrum*, a cerebral theatre quarterly. They didn't pay writers, but participation was an endorsement of something timely, a thing nicely placed in the moment of a movement. I pitched an interview with Linda Griffiths. I had read things before where she had talked about the *game* versus the *religion* of theatre; she talked about performance as a conscious art; she said things that I liked. And of course she was also Maggie, and she was Pierre, and she was Lianna, and she was a hot ticket in New York, and she could have been a movie star but she came back home to work. She was a patriot. She was a hero. I don't remember any of her answers or any of my questions. The interview was published, so it's out there somewhere. What I mostly remember is thinking, *what is this place she's requested we meet*? This place where she lunches daily. These old men and their espressos. These pool tables. What is this Bar Italia? What is this writer's life she leads? This scoundrel, this giant, this artist. Shortly after this meeting I contacted her to perform at a benefit. I'm sure she imagined the interview was a ruse to get her to do another fucking benefit. As I remember, she read from her *roman à clef*, a tale of the theatre, her *Answered Prayers* never published. After that, once a month or so, we'd run into one another at openings and chat and dish. Occasionally we'd be at the same parties, but we wouldn't hang out—I was a drinker and she smoked pot. She came to my shows. She liked my moxie. She saw me as a person who knew how to get things done. Which is why in 2007 she invited me into her kitchen for tea to ask if I would help her develop a film version of *Alien Creature*. It strikes me now as an excellent idea, but I was out of love with the movie world at that time, so I encouraged her to come up with something else. She spoke about this play with the working title *The Odd Women* that no one would ever produce, about getting out of the theatre altogether, about *how do you make a TV show*, and finally she mentioned a radio thing; she was writing a doc for the CBC, on spec, about her father, *the old bastard*, something called *The Last Dog of War*.

***

When Linda played her father, this was the best of Linda too. How she would inhabit and comment at the same time. Playing bitter *and* affectionate. *Resigned*. Resigned was deep in Linda's wheelhouse. *The Last Dog of War* became a tour we did together: Edmonton, two stops in Nova Scotia, Ottawa, Calgary, Montreal, a couple of nights in Toronto. The first night in Toronto was the first night of the show. The day before, Linda had arrived home after having spent a week travelling with her father in the north of England where they attended the last reunion of his RAF WWII squadron. Tonight she would present her recounting of the trip as *The Last Dog of War*. We managed to assemble the promise of a sizable audience. That day she improvised. I structured. She scribbled notes. I made some sound cues. We hung a couple of lights. She did it. It was good. It was funny. Linda was magnetic. The audience loved her. We had the opportunity to do it close to fifty times. But it never really worked. And that was me. I had insisted on a tone of reconciliation at the end of the tale. Resignation wasn't enough, I felt. She fought me on it because it wasn't accurate, but I was adamant that we needed emotional closure, narrative. I said that wanting something to happen was the same as something happening. She indulged me, but she always knew it wasn't true.

***

In rehearsal one will often hear talk of *want*. An actor is expected to want something. It is this verb of *want* that breeds all the other verbs that an actor is expected to engage with to get the wanted thing. The process of determining these verbs and the actor's movement through a scene from line to line, from beat to beat, is known as actioning: *I appeal, I beg, I ignore, I retreat, I advance, I flatter* . . . and on and on. In my experience of Linda this was not her way. For Linda this concept lived in the land of the Holy Narrative—old fashioned, *traditional*. Linda was a person of the new theatre, the theatre without walls. And Linda's spirit not only embodied narrative but *want* as well. Want was not a verb for Linda, it was a noun. She did not have to invent want, to generate want. She lived want. Want and all of its conflict: messy and noble and grand and base and desperate and divine. She was want.

***

First, to me now, she is as she is on the poster for *Lianna*. Iconic Linda. When she comes to my mind's eye, this is more and more how. Not the cultivated blue-black bob in the sharp-lined caricature she used as a headshot. She's become young again. A frizzy-haired beauty, looking deep into something. Being observed. Desire. A question about to come. And, second, she is the opening of *Lianna*. Listen to her voice at the very beginning, off screen, we hear her before we see her. There is a laugh. She's laughing at us. She knows we're there. She knows we can hear her. She knows that's the trick. Stars above, stars below.

"THIS ISN'T THE STORY I SET OUT TO TELL": WORLD WAR II, PROCESS, AND AUTOBIOGRAPHY IN LINDA GRIFFITHS'S *THE LAST DOG OF WAR*

AMANDA ATTRELL

Anomalous in Griffiths's canon as an autobiographical play, *The Last Dog of War* nevertheless exemplifies concerns she explored throughout her career. She was initially inspired to write a historical play about World War II based on a trip with her father: an idea grounded in her career-long dedication to writing about real people and her roots in collective creation. To achieve her goal, Griffiths used a creative process she had developed over the course of her career, improvising this play in front of audiences across Canada and working through her actor self, using improvisation rather than writing. While she performed this play and made alterations to the script, Griffiths also relied upon her audience by bringing them into the performance as her family. This relationship allowed her to move away from an effort to claim historical truth toward being comfortable enough to share more personal realities about the trip and herself. The drafts and transcripts of her various performances, along with the final script as it performs its own process of creation, show us the evolution of Griffiths's focus, which ultimately alights upon her own autobiographical self. By considering the archival traces of the play's creation, we can see how the historical foundations of *The Last Dog of War* and the playwright's personal additions to the script were transformed into an autobiographical portrait of Griffiths herself, with the audience playing a key role in this evolution.[1]

GRIFFITHS'S HISTORIES AND
THE LAST DOG OF WAR

Throughout her career Linda Griffiths experimented with improvisational methods stemming from her roots in collective creation, always moving between the roles of improvising actor and playwright as well as blurring the binary of process and product. She began her work at 25th Street Theatre in Saskatchewan with a focus on her aspirations as an actor. Desiring roles such as Ophelia or Juliet, she acted in plays like Andras Tahn's adaptation of *The Ballad of Billy the Kid* ("Linda Griffiths on Saskatoon").[2] She discovered her inclination and ability to write her own parts while participating in such collective creations as *If You're So Good, Why Are You In Saskatoon?* and *Paper Wheat.* Considering this stage in her career and her "education," she often returned to improvisational methods in order to create, but also became comfortable with what she called the loneliness of writing by herself. As she continued to develop as a playwright, Griffiths maintained a focus on process, frequently writing and speaking about the work of creating her plays.[3] In fact, Griffiths approached *The Last Dog of War* with a focus on process, considering this play a "challenge . . . to do something immediate, raw, and unwriterly"

---

1   For clarity's sake I will use "Linda" to refer to the protagonist of *The Last Dog of War* and Linda Griffiths or Griffiths to speak about the playwright and actor outside of the narrative.

2   Griffiths discusses her time at 25th Street Theatre with Andrew Moodie in a video for Theatre Museum Canada's Legend Library series. Specifically, she tells him, "I thought all I wanted to do was be a kind of dreamy Ophelia or a dreamy Juliet; I wasn't doing that at all."

3   See, for example, Griffiths's interviews with Andrew Moodie ("Playwright Linda Griffiths"), Judith Rudakoff, Muriel Leeper, and Kathleen Gallagher or her articles in *Theatre and AutoBiography: Writing and Performing Lives in Theory and Practice* ("I Am a Thief") and *Canadian Theatre Review* ("Process?"). A recording of her lecture at the SOULO Theatre Festival, given the year she passed away, can be found on YouTube ("LINDA GRIFFITHS ~ Talks About").

after working on *Age of Arousal* via a solitary writer's process ("*The Last Dog of War*: A History of the Process of Development" 1).

Her initial impulse to create *The Last Dog of War* related not only to her career-long focus on process, but also to her tendency to write plays starring non-fictional characters. This concern developed on multiple levels, both historical and personal. Griffiths begins her essay "I Am a Thief . . . Not Necessarily Honourable Either," featured in the anthology *Theatre and AutoBiography*, with the bald statement, "I've never written a biographical play," arguing that biographies are "a literary model" disconnected from her theatrical approach (301, 303). However, she acknowledges that *Maggie & Pierre*, *Jessica*, *The Duchess*, and *Alien Creature: a visitation from Gwendolyn MacEwen* were all "inspired by (admittedly) real people" (301). *The Last Dog of War* is another play based on a non-fictional character—or rather, on two; Griffiths's initial concept was to focus on her father and his participation in WWII, but as she developed her idea it evolved into a depiction of herself.

When Griffiths wrote about how her education in collective creation and her tendency to focus on non-fictional people influenced her work, the audience also often entered into her reflections. For example, "I Am a Thief" deviates from these subjects to contemplate how her process took the audience into account. She reveals that she considered what her audience would know about Wallis Simpson, deciding how much information to give them in *The Duchess*. Similarly, while creating *Alien Creature*, she "felt the connection between [Gwendolyn MacEwen and herself] was so strong, [she] took the chance the audience would feel it" (305). Unmistakably, MacEwen and Griffiths blur together in this play. For example, the text's first moments have Gwendolyn coming on stage, "*looking at the audience, as if drinking them in*" and saying, "You're so beautiful [. . .] You look like. . . . people sitting in an audience. You're very precious to me" (*Alien Creature* 13). Discerning between the voices of the actor, the playwright, and the character proves difficult in this moment, as in many others in Griffiths's oeuvre. Griffiths even argued, while discussing her responsibility as a playwright and actor in *Jessica*, *Maggie & Pierre*, and *Alien Creature* that "when other actors do my work, that basic connection between the material and the audience isn't there" ("I Am a Thief"

305). In "Process?" she comes to the conclusion that performing "without a net in front of audiences . . . is the best way to get around the traps inherent in literary material" (61). Although process and writing about real people are central to her oeuvre, Griffiths's connection to and relationship with her audience also influenced much of her work.

These three aspects each play an important role in how Griffiths creates an autobiographic self in *The Last Dog of War*. Autobiography necessarily entails the subject creating him or herself, as Jenn Stephenson acknowledges in *Performing Autobiography: Contemporary Canadian Drama* when she muses on a sketch that depicts a man being drawn, with the man himself holding the pen (3). In *The Last Dog of War*, Griffiths likewise draws herself as Linda. Leigh Gilmore's autobiographics, a "genealogy of the feminist interpretive strategy," sheds light upon the process by which Griffiths achieves this effect (5). Building upon the work of Michel Foucault, Gilmore explains:

> Genealogy must find its subject in the act of seeking it, for history itself is part of the historicity of genealogical inquiry. Unlike historical inquiry, which already knows everything important about its subject and situation, "genealogy operates on a field of entangled and confused parchments, on documents that have been scratched over and recopied many times." (5)

Just so, Griffiths's process in *The Last Dog of War* led her from a historical focus to one resembling a genealogical act of seeking. For example, while describing the negotiations and research that led to the trip with her father, Linda draws from a suitcase "*large Second World War books and . . . begins to unpack them and pile them up in order to sit on them*" (*Last Dog* 10).[4] Instead of opening these history books and reporting on their content, she sits on them, just as this story turned into something other than a history: a "dilemma," as she reveals in the second sentence of the play (3). True to herself as a playwright and actor, she takes this "dilemma . . . to the theatre" (3).

---

4 All citations to the play, unless otherwise noted, come from the 2016 published book.

Rather than relying upon how history has been previously told and how her career has been represented by others, Linda uses her own history to create an autobiographical self in this play.

Writing about *Alien Creature*, Katherine McLeod has approached the biographical impulse of Griffiths's work through Gilmore's concept of auto-biographics as well as her own theory of performative mirror talk, which she defines as the "method of auto/biographic representation that foregrounds its own *process* of making . . . a *self* in flux" (141; emphasis in original). *The Last Dog of War* was created with similar improvisational methods to those that gave birth to *Alien Creature*; perhaps for that reason, it too contains what McLeod dubs "a *performative* interaction between [Griffiths] and her subject" (142; emphasis in original). In *The Last Dog of War*, however, rather than writing and representing a biographical character as both playwright and actor, Griffiths uses performative mirror talk to create her own autobi-ographical self. She developed this autobiographical representation during her improvised performances, so that the "audience is intimately part of this process of performing a self—a self that," as McLeod further describes, "rever-berates somewhere within this negotiatory process between performer and audience" (142).

Although *The Last Dog of War* has been published in a final form, Griffiths's truest creation of her self arguably exists in its multiple iterations and drafts, and in its own re-performance during each remount of this play. The self the audience sees in these contexts is "opposed to a search for ori-gins even as it traces the temporary homes of meaning in a general attempt to understand where truth comes from" (Gilmore 6). Griffiths's move away from a historical narrative claiming truth toward a text that performs its own process of creation leads to Linda's autobiographical representation of herself, sitting on history books and wearing a pink leather jacket with a Royal Air Force leather helmet and goggles (*Last Dog*, Playwrights 22). Griffiths also places herself in the audience by considering how she becomes a spectator of her father's reunion: "I realize that we're all lined up like an audience and I'm wearing a pink leather jacket" (38). Linda notices and points out that from the research stage of this story she, along with her family, have switched roles and are playing the part of the audience. Moreover, while researching this play based on history, she remains herself by continuing to wear her own costume. Throughout the process of the play's creation—the process that led to Griffiths's creation of an autobiographical self—she was mindful of her own fluid role and of her connection with the audience.

THE LAST DOG OF WAR AS (NON-)HISTORY PLAY

The inspiration of *The Last Dog of War* lies in a trip Griffiths made with her father: one originally related in her mind to the relatively traditional aim of writing a historical play. Searching for inspiration, she accompanied her father to his World War II Royal Air Force squadron's "last reunion" (9). Her initial goal was to "do this [play] in stages on the way to the History Channel," and she shares with the audience her planned course of action: "First CBC Radio . . . Put together some interviews" (10). In the end, however, their trip became a one-woman show written and performed by Griffiths, with her performing solo as "Linda" (3). Linda spends the majority of the play telling the audience about her time at the reunion, which she calls "Mission Reunion," describing the various events as "targets" (12, 32). She focuses a great deal on her journey with her father, including their moments of "negotiating" with one another about their trip (12). The pair's time spent in England with relatives Wilf and Elizabeth, their inability to register for the reunion, and Linda's discovery of her "roots" are also recounted in the play (30).

The historical aspirations of *The Last Dog of War* remain visible in the final published script despite its development beyond Griffiths's initial aspirations. Linda regales the audience with satires about her father's time as a wireless operator/air gunner and with details about the war. For example, "*pac[ing] in front of the stage, like a lecturer,*" she explains "the difference between a Spitfire and a Lancaster. Between Fighter Command and Bomber Command" (20–21). The audience learns her father served in Bomber Command on a Lancaster, "a big, heavy bomber" that dropped bombs on "targets" from "military bases, factories" to "houses the workers lived in . . . cities, anywhere people congregated, municipal buildings, squares, theatres" (21–22). Linda shares the reality that the chance of "surviving a tour of duty at this time in the war was one in three," but also acts out the effects of a bombing mission, imitating the sound of civilians on the ground crying "help" and shouting "BURNING" (23, 28). By so doing, she interrogates "the furry comfort of history," asking the audience, "[T]he Second World War was a good war, right? . . . Hitler, the Holocaust—who doesn't hate Nazis?" (20).

These historical lessons become associated with her family's personal history when Linda considers the treatment of Bomber Command after the war. While trying to register for the reunion with her father, Griffiths described herself as a journalist; her original message to D.C. Boughton, a member of the 49th Squadron whose email address she found online, reads, "I'm a Canadian playwright, journalist and actor . . . Do you have any spots reserved for 'the press'?" ("Subject").[5] Quickly discovering her mistake, Griffiths learns that "the 49th Squadron and all of Bomber Command have been vilified [by the press ever] since the war" (*Last Dog* 12)—a fact her father had never shared with her. At first, then, because she has falsely described herself as a member of the press to gain access, Linda is told that "[t]here will be absolutely no press, no journalists allowed. That's it. Thank you very much" (12).

This anecdote leads into Griffiths's first overt act of self-exploration in *The Last Dog of War*. Linda admits to the audience that her email contained a "lie:" "I'm not a journalist. I'm a playwright and an actor" (10). In the transcript of her initial improvised performance, she divulges:

> But you see that is really the first lie . . . I am acting as if I know, as if I've talked to my father, as if we are in tandem . . . Now I have to figure out how I approach this with my father . . . this is how it's always gone—give him nothing, want nothing. But I want something now. I want those stories . . . this is such a leap in our relationship. (*Last Dog*, 2005 5–6)

---

5   In the play, D.C. Boughton's name has been changed to Charles Langley.

Speaking in a stream of consciousness, Griffiths allows the audience to witness her working through her dilemma. Importantly, her act of adding the title of journalist to her identity not only functions as an effort to gain access to the reunion, but also hints at some discomfort with her true role as a Canadian actor and playwright: a point that is furthered in a much later autobiographical addition to the script, in which she tells the audience she "wanted to be an actor—parents hate that" (*Last Dog*, 2011 12). Her discomfort with her own identity stems from her relationship with her father, which in turn affects the feasibility of their shared trip. During the process of creation, *The Last Dog of War* thus transforms from a historical play into a different one, focused on a much more personal story than she had initially "set out to tell" (*Last Dog* 3).

Although Griffiths was inspired by and initially focused on the historical aspects of her narrative, in performance Linda introduces the personal part of their trip together only after describing the process by which the play was created. She also stops to recount a "dream" in which she attempts to tell her father and Clare Coulter about her escape from an exploding bus and responds to his refusal to listen by trying to hit him with a piece of wood that "barely touches his cheek" (3–6). Only after she describes the play's genesis and her dream, which returns near the end of the play, does Linda finally tell the audience, "Here's the idea" (6), and share her goal of writing a historical play. The inspiration for this show lies in its focus on the reunion and World War II, but it also contains personal tangents from the beginning.

PROCESS AS PRODUCT

As *The Last Dog of War* developed over multiple drafts and performances, these personal tangents became ever more essential to the story thanks to Griffiths's reliance upon her collective creation roots as well as her own creative process. Traces of the development of this play exist in various forms, from transcripts and recordings of improvised performances to handwritten notes by Griffiths and more structured typed scripts.[6] The first iteration of the piece was performed impromptu in Theatre Passe Muraille's Mainspace, "possibly [on] a Sunday," which Griffiths improvised based only on ideas and a running order developed with Daniel MacIvor (1). A transcript of this performance survives, covered in Griffiths's handwriting as she edited and adjusted it. Word documents dated 2007, 2009, and 2011 seem to mark three more important iterations of the play as it transformed from an improvised piece to a written script.[7] Each script features Griffiths's notes on both the front and back of the pages, making comments, alterations, and adjustments that resemble the "documents that have been scratched over and recopied many times" referred to by Foucault and Gilmore. The version of *The Last Dog of War* eventually published in 2016 by Playwrights Canada Press is almost identical to the 2011 document with "Final" in its file name. These various versions of the play allow us to understand in detail how Griffiths moved from writing a piece based on a trip with her father toward sharing an increasing amount of personal detail, creating the overtly autobiographical section of the final text in which she discusses her family life and career as a Canadian playwright with the audience.

As the play developed during performances across Canada, Griffiths's concern with process became an integral component of the story. Linda describes the first iteration of *The Last Dog of War* early on in each version of the play. The stage directions in the final published version emphasize the role of travel in her process as Linda "*enters carrying two bags over her shoulders,*" as if she has just gotten off the plane (3). These props also signal to the audience that although the trip was meant to be research for a historical play she now carries physical and emotional baggage from this voyage, which she

6   Many of these documents and recordings are held as a part of the Canadian Theatre Archives in McLaughlin Library at the University of Guelph. I was also graciously sent material on this play by Griffiths's agent, Michael Petrasek, and want to thank Charlotte Corbeil-Coleman for making these resources accessible.

7   Even within these years there are multiple versions of the script with different dates. I cite one draft from each year to maintain consistency. Additionally, while there are large differences between each year, the changes made close together are more nuanced.

has brought with her onto the stage (3). She describes her first performance of the piece as her "one uncensored blah," which she "was never going to do . . . again" (3). However, this one night led to performances across Canada, from Nova Scotia to Calgary, Vancouver, and then Winnipeg, where "suddenly it was a show" (4).[8] Griffiths's process of creation thus became an important part of the play itself, present from the first impromptu performance.

The initial concept for *The Last Dog of War* was grounded in an approach not dissimilar to the collective creation methodology Griffiths had learnt from artists such as Paul Thompson in the early years of her career (Rudakoff 27). She conceived the play as "an experiment in process inspired by her improvisational roots" ("*The Last Dog of War*: A History" 1). It was to be "composed of the discovery process itself," as Diane Bessai says of *The Farm Show*, directed by Thompson, in which the audience is "invited to participate in the same process of discovery as" the actor (67). However, while working on, writing, and performing the script, Griffiths began to depart from established approaches to collective creation, working instead with her own improvisational and creative methods. Indeed, this play represents a further exploration of her connection to the audience and her own process of creation.

In "Process?," published in 1998, Griffiths attempts to define what this term encompasses. She questions if process refers to "improvising a play . . . writing . . . collaborating with directors, other writers, [or] audiences," as well as exploring if it includes "what happens behind closed doors in the rehearsal room or . . . what the audience sees" (57). Griffiths decides that when it comes to her work, she is "talking about all of these things and more" (57). Process to her was creating as both an actor and playwright, although she made a distinction between her creative process doing "utter free-form work" stemming from her actor self, and her more literary creative process on the plays that were primarily grounded in her writing (57). At the time she wrote "Process?," Griffiths was creating *Alien Creature*, about Canadian

---

8   The published version of *The Last Dog of War* states the play "was first fully produced by Theatre Projects Manitoba from November 5 through 14, 2009, at the Costume Museum of Canada in Winnipeg, Manitoba" (1).

poet Gwendolyn MacEwen: the first time she tried performing "without a net in front of audiences" by "improvis[ing] in fifteen-minute segments at events through the city over the course of a year" (61). The only other time she used this method of creation was while developing *The Last Dog of War*.

In the end, Griffiths's process for this play involved a combination of her two previous improvisational methods; she did not rely solely upon the traditional collective format of actors improvising while a director watches and arranges the play, nor did she duplicate her own earlier approach of performing small pieces of a text in front of an audience. In a document entitled "*The Last Dog of War*: A History of the Process of Development" from Griffiths's website, she acknowledges that her use of improvisation was "inspired by years of doing collective creations with Paul Thompson" (1).[9] This document also contains a discussion of Daniel MacIvor's title of "buddy" during the improvised initial performance: a role that is "both/neither director/dramaturge," which Griffiths herself created as part of her theatre company, Duchess Productions (1). Although MacIvor's role ultimately became that of director and dramaturge, the play began with Griffiths's own process of relying on MacIvor as her buddy and on the "primal relationship between actor and audience" (1). Griffiths's choice to ask MacIvor to play this role represents a conscious decision to rely on her own ideas about process. Furthermore, as she continued performing across Canada, the transformation from improvised piece to text occurred in front of an audience, with the audience becoming part of the play as well.

THE AUDIENCE AS COLLABORATOR

Griffiths's process was deeply connected to her roots as both playwright and actor, but *The Last Dog of War* became more personal thanks to this performer/audience relationship. The different versions of its ending demonstrate how Griffiths's relationship with her audience led to two notable alterations to the play's resolution. The transcript of the initial 2005 impromptu performance

---

9   Since Griffiths's passing in 2014 this website is no longer available.

begins and ends with "the dream."[10] Daniel MacIvor helped Griffiths structure the show by putting together a running order for this first performance,
and together they decided that if a dream sequence began the play, it should
also end it. Although these two seasoned playwrights thought bookending
the play with this dream would work best, Griffiths's reliance upon her audience eventually led her to conclude the play in a much more personal way.
Griffiths noted that during this first performance the audience spontaneously
applauded at a different point, which she realized "*should have been the end*";
she asked, "*How would I have known except for them*?" ("*The Last Dog of
War*: A History" 2; emphasis in original). She later wrote on a transcript of
this performance, "It's not war I love, it's not war," adding this line after the
dream (2005 32). This alteration makes the play's conclusion an overtly personal revelation rather than relying upon the dream, which does not make
a clear statement about her relationship with her father. The line she added
also revisits a concept Linda introduces when speaking about her family at
the beginning of the play: "There is something I have to confess to you—I
love war" (2005 1). Each subsequent script ranging from this 2005 version
to the 2011 document has the new ending, and the final published version
from 2016 ends with Linda saying, "It's not war that I love" followed by a "*[s]
low fade to black*" (40), clearly concluding that during this trip she realized
her love for her father. Griffiths did not document at what moment of her
impromptu performance the audience applauded or what she felt needed to
be changed, but it is clear from these alterations that as Griffiths made "the
transition from informal improvisor to precise performer" in front of audiences, it led to adjustments that increased the intimacy of the script ("*The
Last Dog of War*: A History" 3).

   Another significant alteration to the ending, which also built upon
Griffiths's awareness of the performer/audience relationship, is the removal

---

10   The typed text of this document reads, "This is a transcript of the improvised night
on July 4, 2005" (1). However, "*The Last Dog of War*: A History" begins with, "In April
2006, Linda Griffiths resolved to attend the reunion with her father" (1). Indeed, there
is an inconsistency in the documentation of this trip, which leaves its dates in question.
However, because the transcript does clearly state 2005 I will honour this date.

of a section present in an early version of the play, titled "Merlin and N[i]mue" ("Last dog order" 1). The 2005 transcript reveals that near the end of this impromptu performance Linda tells the audience about "Merlin the Enchanter" and his "girlfriend" with whom he shares all his spells before the end of his life (31). Ultimately, "Merlin doesn't die . . . he is just in a coma. With the memory of having had all this power taken by Nimue" (31). Linda ends the tale: "In the story that I know, Merlin forgives Nimue for pulling out the stories, for draining him in the process, because he knows that she will come (home?)" (31). Griffiths's use of this mythological story serves as a metaphor for her own working through the guilt she feels about telling her father's stories. However, this story veils Griffiths's own personal struggle, which she discusses more openly with the audience in later versions of the play.

By her own admission, a strategy Griffiths had developed for writing about real people was to "always place in [her] mind's eye the people themselves in the audience" ("I Am a Thief" 305). This strategy of imagining her subject in the audience during her creative process was learnt not from collective creation, but during her work writing *Jessica*, a play about the life of Maria Campbell.[11] This experience was the first time that Griffiths wrote about a subject who was also a member of her audience. Campbell accused her of stealing, bidding her "[a]dmit that you're a thief and give back tenfold" (Bessai 230; Gallagher and Griffiths 127). "[S]tealing, transform[ing], and giv[ing] back tenfold" became a dedication Griffiths maintained throughout her career (Griffiths and Gallagher 127). By imagining her father in the audience of *The Last Dog of War*, Griffiths challenged herself to speak about "true things" and to include more intimate details in each iteration of the script (*Last Dog* 4). In the final version, she reflects on putting her father in the audience, "I don't know how this will change what you see tonight, but

---

11   While Maria Campbell and Linda Griffiths initially worked with Paul Thompson on this project, it ultimately veered away from the method of collective creation. Instead, it was Griffiths who spent time with Campbell researching for the play before performing the lead role then reworking the script herself years later (Griffiths and Campbell 10). The tumultuous process of this play is discussed at length in *The Book of Jessica*, and is examined in Jacqueline Petropoulos's essay elsewhere in this volume.

I believe it will" (4). Perhaps the idea of her father's presence gave Griffiths licence to tell his stories in public, giving back to him by relying upon her connection to the audience, whom she treated as though they were themselves members of her family.

This approach becomes increasingly accentuated in each version of *The Last Dog of War*. In the April 2007 version, Griffiths follows the opening dream sequence and explanation of the concept of the play by telling the audience,

> The trouble is the reality of talking about these things is a bit different from how I imagined it. So I thought that if you could become my relatives . . . then I would be able to say whatever I need to say. I could betray. If I have to. (2–3)

Naming and describing her relatives Jennifer and Wilf, as well as his wife Elizabeth, she points to members of the audience who could become these family members or "miscellaneous younger cousins" (3), all parts of her extended family, with whom she is not intimately connected. In a script from February 2009, Linda adopts the audience as family at the same point, but gives them the option of playing more closely related family members. She tells the audience they may be her brother, Bruce, or even her father. She also expands upon her struggle with telling this story about her father and her feelings of dishonesty, revealing, "I've tried different things, like imagining him in the audience and I just can't go there" (2009 2). By 2011, after performing this play in front of audiences for five years, when Griffiths asks them to become her family, she adds, "And then, and this is pretty loaded, there's my father, I'm going to place him right there" (4). Although Griffiths had felt unable to conjure the figure of her father in previous performances, by relying upon her audience she eventually became able to tell this deeply personal story by doing just that. Clearly, the audience was part of the process that allowed Griffiths to explore her career-spanning concerns about writing and performing characters based on real people.

A comparison of Griffiths's various drafts reveals that as she came to depend on her audience she also incorporated an increasing amount of autobiographical material, leaving more of herself on stage and in the text. Initially, Griffiths only provides information about herself necessary to the story at hand. For example, in the 2007 script Linda states, "War was part of my childhood . . . War was the currency in our house" (4). Although these are personal details, they function to introduce the trip to England with her father. Between the 2007 and 2009 versions, Griffiths made this section more detailed by including autobiographical information unrelated to war. She talks about the period when she decided to become an actor and about the start of her career: "Then I hit puberty . . . wanted to become an actor, I got kicked out of theatre school, but then something happened to me . . . I got famous, through my own stuff" (2009 3). Between the 2009 and published versions of *The Last Dog of War*, Griffiths further enhanced this autobiographical section, making it more detailed. What is more, she adopted a conversational tone as Linda tells the audience, "[S]omething happened to me, something that every young actor dreams of. I got famous. You didn't know I was famous? I was. And through my own work" (7). Griffiths became best known for *Maggie & Pierre* and her collaborations with Paul Thompson, but she also won many awards for her solo work as both writer and actor. With this direct statement, she makes it clear how she wishes her career to be seen: it should not be defined by her roots in collective creation, but by the powerful plays she wrote on her own. She also shares that while she was successful for a while, "[T]his is Canada, [and] it gets harder and harder till finally I'm desperate, I'm broke, I'm a PLAYWRIGHT, my last play has gone down like a turd in a punch bowl—*Chronic*, maybe you've heard about it? No? A good play. And I have no ideas" (7). In this version of the play, Linda admits that her idea for *The Last Dog of War* came from this point of desperation in her career. The audience also becomes privy to her application for funding so she can afford to go on the trip: "The CBC is always good for a thou, right? And a good tape recorder?" (10). With this statement, which remains relatively similar in each version of the script, Linda shares the reality of working in Canadian theatre. By exposing her own visceral, vulnerable connection to the theatre—and to her audience—Griffiths moves from her initial historical idea toward the creation and performance of her self.

The final version's ending accentuates the importance of the audience to this process of self-creation and self-performance. After a day of attending reunion events, Linda visits a war memorial along with her father, cousin Wilf, and Elizabeth. She "think[s] of all the blood that was spilt there" until she sees her father putting on "his blue blazer with the medals so he can have his picture taken" (39). The first photo she calls "standard—it's Dad in the rec room at Christmas" (39). However, Linda says the second photo was special, demonstrating for the audience her father's pose: "*Linda cocks her head, grins, and bends over on one leg, one arm on her waist, in a classic dashing flyer pose*" (39). As she continues narrating, "I take the picture," a camera flash comes from behind the audience before she says, "But then, you, my family. You know that. You were there" (40). The choice to have the flash occur behind the audience makes their relationship with Griffiths even more intimate, as this moment reminds them that they have been embodying her family throughout the play. Now they embody *her*, taking the photo as Griffiths did, while she plays her father. Significantly, this lighting change is not explicit in a script until the "Final" 2011 version (21). Like the play itself, this moment develops from Griffiths's musings about historical events. She then depends on her audience to play an important role in the story, that of taking the picture, just as she relied on them to help her perform and transform this play. Linda then speaks honestly in her final line when she reveals, "It's not war that I love," directly addressing her family, her audience, with a genuine moment of self-performance and concluding a play whose process chronicles her creation of this autobiographical self (40). The archival traces of the ending, and this deeply intimate conclusion, prove that the play's initial subject of World War II was transformed by Griffiths's relationship with her audience into a focus on its own process of creation.

This moment also breaks down the binaries between author and subject as well as between performer and audience that Linda/Griffiths has been playing with since the first moments of the play. It echoes her earlier musings about the performer/audience binary when Linda and her family watched the official reunion. As McLeod argues of *Alien Creature*, Griffiths's use of improvisation to create and perform herself in *The Last Dog of War* "allows us to consider how self-representations that emerge through performative mirror talk continue to be in flux—not only because they are expressed through the ever-shifting medium of speech but also because of their continued engagement with the representational process itself" (141). Similar to the intertwining voices of MacEwen, Griffiths the performer, and Griffiths the playwright in *Alien Creature*, the audience's intertwining with Linda in the conclusion of *The Last Dog of War* demonstrates the fluidity of self. It emphasizes that all of the roles in the play—playwright, performer, characters, and audience members—have been in flux throughout the development of Griffiths's autobiographical self. This text's preoccupations are "the basic connections of theatre—the playwright and the performer, the actor and the character, the character and the audience, the individual and her community," as Jenn Stephenson writes about solo performance ("Introduction" xiii). Although Griffiths investigated these connections throughout her career, this play became her ultimate exploration of herself and her creative process, conflating all of these roles. As her family, we the audience experience this entire adventure and the process with Linda, getting to know her as daughter, actor, playwright, and family member.

   The Last Dog of War tells a story about World War II, another story about the process of its own creation, and a third about the construction of Linda Griffiths's autobiographical self. In the end, however, it is difficult to distinguish between these disparate components, for Griffiths is present in each element of this play, working through a number of concerns that were central to her career. Griffiths first imagined *The Last Dog of War* as an opportunity to write about history, envisioning her research and future performance as an experiment tied to her roots in collective creation. However, as she continued to perform this narrative for audiences across Canada, her own process and methods of creating plays about real people changed the story. Bringing the audience into each performance as her family, Griffiths ultimately collaborated with them, experimenting with "impulse and immediacy" ("*The Last Dog of War*: A History" 1). The differences between her various drafts demonstrate her expansion of the more personal aspects of this play. In the 2007 script, Linda begins by thanking the audience for coming, describes the development of the play, and states, "Everything in it is true" (3). In the 2011 version, she opens by admitting, "This isn't the story I set out to tell" (3). Her reliance "upon the primal relationship between actor and audience" had transformed her text ("*The Last Dog of War*: A History" 1). Ultimately, although this play "isn't the story [she] set out to tell," it contains within its entanglement of historical and personal narrative a precious autobiographical representation of herself, her dedication to the theatre, and her love of her audience (3).

RE-VIEWING *JESSICA* AND *THE BOOK OF JESSICA:* CRITICAL AND CULTURAL TRANSFORMATIONS

JACQUELINE PETROPOULOS

When *Jessica: A Theatrical Transformation* was produced in 1986, audiences in Toronto, Ottawa, and Quebec City flocked to see the award-winning play critics were calling an "innovative," "moving," and "courageous" exploration of a Métis woman's search for identity. Praising the play for its cultural authenticity, the mainstream press welcomed what it believed to be a true-to-life narrative that had finally broken through the barriers of racism that haunted Canada's recent theatrical past. As Barbara Crook of *The Ottawa Citizen* put it, *Jessica* offered "Canada's native actors" an opportunity to play "realistic, major roles in mainstream productions . . . after years of playing token Indians and perpetuating stereotypes." The publication of Linda Griffiths's and Maria Campbell's *The Book of Jessica: A Theatrical Transformation* just three years later challenged this interpretation, however. Unlike the emphasis in the theatre reviews on the casting of Indigenous performers in believable roles, *The Book of Jessica* exposed the hidden relations of power behind the representation on stage by looking at the personal conflicts and political tensions between the text's white and Métis collaborators. In effect outing Griffiths for voice appropriation, scholars have since analyzed *The Book of Jessica* for the ways in which it both critiques and ironically reproduces colonialist relations of power. This shift from discourses of cultural authenticity toward charges of cultural appropriation has since given way to new scholarship on *The Book of Jessica* as a contested site of cross-cultural collaboration. By tracing the critical contexts that have shaped interpretations of both *Jessica* and *The Book of Jessica*, I argue that shifting political views of identity and representation have been intimately linked to the reception of both works. The book's subtitle, "A Theatrical Transformation," aptly describes the process by which these texts have themselves transformed, and been transformed by, changing social and cultural discourses.

Written in 1989, *The Book of Jessica* includes the 1986 version of *Jessica* as well as a discussion of the process behind the creation of the play. Rather than provide a linear narrative to contextualize the dramatic text, the book tells this story through a combination of chronology, narration, and dialogue taken from taped conversations between Griffiths and Campbell. The reader learns that *Jessica* began as a collective creation under the direction of Paul Thompson but later morphed into a co-authored piece by Campbell, Griffiths, and Thompson. This play was produced at Saskatoon's 25th Street Theatre in 1982,[1] and was later revised by Griffiths for production at Toronto's Theatre Passe Muraille in 1986. By billing the revised work as a play written by Linda Griffiths "in collaboration with Maria Campbell," Griffiths displaced Campbell from her role as co-author of a play based on her own life, relegating her to an undefined subordinate status. *The Book of Jessica* details how Campbell felt marginalized and alienated throughout the process of creating the play, but even more so when Griffiths rewrote the text on her own, only asking for Campbell's input after the fact. She accuses Griffiths of stealing her thoughts, her life story, and her culture. She compares Griffiths to "the man in Ottawa who writes the Indian Act, then comes to the people after it's done and asks for their blessing and input" (81). *The Book of Jessica* painfully re-enacts the tensions, wounds, and frustrations of the two collaborators, framing this story within colonial relations of power and appropriation. Campbell attempts to heal these injuries by demanding that Griffiths take greater accountability for her actions, but this reconciliation is never fully achieved by a narrative that remains provisional, ambivalent, and open-ended.

---

1   The playscript lists 1981 as the production date, but the timeline at the front of the book gives 1982 as the date of production. Historical sources, such as the "*25th Street Theatre Collection*" by Glen Makahonuk and Diane Bessai's *Playwrights of Collective Creation*, confirm the 1982 date.

Critics and audiences of the 1986 productions of *Jessica* were unaware of this backstory and the charges of appropriation that would surface three years later. However, this lack of information does not justify or explain why none of the reviewers questioned the right of a white author to tell a Métis woman's story. This glaring oversight in the critical reception of *Jessica*, as compared with the radically different approach of *The Book of Jessica*, suggests that an important shift had taken place in cultural discourses of identity and representation during the brief time span between the play's production in 1986 and the book's publication in 1989. While this ideological blind spot in the critical discourse clearly betrays a lack of sensitivity to questions of appropriation, the 1986 reviews focus on the Indigenous performers rather than the writer of the script to construct a narrative of cultural authenticity. That is, they neatly sidestep the question of authorship altogether by looking to the visual representation on stage as a marker of cultural truth and legitimacy.

To a certain extent, the critical reception of *Jessica* was progressive for its time, supporting a newly emergent discourse of identity politics that focused on increased visibility for marginalized subjects in order to promote social change and transformation. Though *Jessica* undoubtedly opened doors for Indigenous performers during a period when they were struggling for greater representation in the theatre—bolstering the careers of many important and influential Indigenous theatre artists, such as Tantoo Cardinal, Monique Mojica, Makka Kleist, and Graham Greene—the emphasis on performance unfortunately eclipsed the question of authorship. "While there is a deeply ethical appeal in the desire for a more inclusive landscape and certainly under-represented communities can be empowered by enhanced visibility," Peggy Phelan cautions that a "more nuanced relationship to the power of visibility needs to be pursued" than the discourse of identity politics imagines (7). Visibility politics, as Phelan warns, often fetishizes visual representations as signs of truth without pausing to consider the relations of power hidden from view. Similarly, reviews of *Jessica* that celebrate the casting of Indigenous women take their presence as verifiable, visible proof of the cultural authenticity of the theatrical narrative. More so than Campbell's involvement in the project, the casting of Tantoo Cardinal and later Monique Mojica as Jessica for

productions in Toronto and Ottawa cemented the widespread critical interpretation of the play as a truthful reflection of the life experiences of a Métis
woman. In order to support this reading, critics conflate the identity of the
character with that of the actor, arguing, more or less, that there is no real difference between Jessica and the Indigenous women who performed the role on
stage. This line of reasoning reproduces an essentialist logic that homogenizes
and naturalizes race as a biological essence. The title of Bill Taylor's article
for *The Toronto Star* says it all: "Mojica's Role Her Birthright." As if this large,
bold-faced headline weren't enough, the opening line declares that "[t]he fan
who ran after Monique Mojica in the street, yelling, 'Jessica! Jessica!' Wasn't
too far off the mark." By insisting that Mojica *is* Jessica, Taylor views the performance of identity on stage as an authentic reflection of the real rather than
a theatrical representation. Various reviews of Tantoo Cardinal's performance
of Jessica also reinforce this essentialist interpretation. According to Brian
Johnson of *Maclean's*, for instance, "Cardinal dons the title role of Jessica like
a *second skin*" (63; my emphasis). Similarly, Robert Crew of *The Toronto Star*
claims "the play Jessica [*sic*] fits her [Cardinal] like a glove."

   This inverted logic, which takes the real-life identity of the performer as
proof of the authenticity of the theatrical representation, confirms Phelan's
point that the discourse of identity politics puts too much faith in the visual
field as a mode of truth-telling and truth-making. At its worst, this recourse
to visibility politics surreptitiously reinforces the essentialist belief that physical markers such as skin colour or sexual characteristics serve as accurate
reflections of one's "real" identity and that members of marginalized groups
can be easily and unproblematically lumped together (Phelan 7). Indeed, by
describing the role of Jessica as a "second skin" and "birthright," and equating
it with the identities of the three very different Indigenous women involved
in the play, the newspaper reviews construct an oversimplified and homog-
enized view of Indigeneity. Ironically, the critic who insists Jessica *is* Mojica,
also quotes Mojica as saying, "Maria is Métis, Jessica is Métis. I am not Métis.
I'm a half-breed but not a Métis" (Taylor). Though Mojica openly distances
herself from the part she plays on stage by pointing to the cultural differences
between and among Indigenous people, the article as a whole reproduces the

reductionist logic that tacitly invites members of the dominant white society to view all Indigenous women as essentially the same.

By assuming that the play's protagonist reflects the real-life identity of the performer, the reviews also fail to critique the legitimacy of a role that was written by a white playwright. Griffiths not only wrote the part, she was the first to perform the role of Jessica in 1982. Griffiths admits that she felt uncomfortable about the appropriative aspects of this performance when she reveals in *The Book of Jessica* that she "brown[ed] up" to play the part, and worried about the "image of [herself] on stage in brown greasepaint and borrowed feathers" (54, 53). She goes on to explain that her "sense of guilt over playing Jessica" later became "an obsession" when she was criticized "not for [her] performance, but for [her] position, racially, in the play" by "white liberals" (54, 53). This criticism may seem obvious today, but prior to the 1980s it was common for white women to play Indigenous characters on mainstream stages in works by white authors, including most notably Frances Hyland in the title role of George Ryga's 1967 play *The Ecstasy of Rita Joe*.[2] This changed in 1981—just a year before Griffiths's *Jessica*—when a production starring Margo Kane was the first to cast Indigenous performers in all the Indigenous roles (Wasserman, "George" 26). While Griffiths was rightly critiqued during this new turning point in history that paid greater attention to the politics of performing racialized identities, her blatant act of appropriation nevertheless raised the question of whether a white woman should presume to represent an Indigenous character on stage. The casting of Indigenous women in 1986, by contrast, concealed the play's mode of production, helping to authenticate the representation by making it seem natural and real.[3] I am not suggesting

---

2   The original production starred two Indigenous performers, Chief Dan George and August Schellenberg, which "was a sign of progress at the time," according to Jerry Wasserman, but the part of Rita Joe went to Hyland, "a classically trained white actress" ("George" 26).

3   Natalie Alvarez's discussion of "iconicity" offers further insight into this question of casting choices. Drawing on the theories of Elin Diamond, she argues that "'the mimetic property of acting' in which the 'performer's body conventionally resembles the object (or character) to which it refers'" relies on an economy of exchange that "trades on the actor's

that Griffiths should have reprised her role, but that the critical discourse of the mid-1980s was too narrowly focused on the visual field, failing to examine the larger question of who has the right or *author*ity to tell Indigenous stories.[4] Although the press supported an important political goal by celebrating the right of Indigenous performers to portray their own communities on stage, this lack of critical attention to the play's authorship suggests that visibility was seen as the sole marker of social change and progress at the time.

While critics of the 1986 production of *Jessica* had no reason to believe that Campbell did not work on the newly revised script, since it was billed as a play written by Griffiths "in collaboration with Campbell," this does not explain why they deemed it a straightforward and faithful approximation of a Métis woman's point of view, as if the white playwright were a neutral observer with unmediated access to another culture. Aside from the complicated question of whether a fictitious text can ever give us access to an unmediated truth, the critical discourse conveniently overlooked Campbell's marginalized status as Griffiths's collaborator. Together with the casting of Indigenous performers, the simple fact that Campbell was involved at all in the making of *Jessica* was treated as evidence enough to support the widespread critical interpretation of the play as a true-to-life and authentic depiction of cultural identity.

At best, the critical discourse in 1986 gives Campbell secondary status as the play's collaborator, through very brief and oblique references to her role in the creation of a theatrical narrative based on her life. Often, just a

---

body, which becomes 'laminated' to the character in the convention [that] semioticians [call] 'iconicity'" (154). On the one hand, when white actors play non-white parts, this disrupts the illusion of reality and provides a useful index for asking "what [went] wrong." On the other hand, "the appeal for continuity between actor and character in the logic of iconicity [sometimes] runs the risk of re-entrenching essentialized representations" and masking differences due to "the expectation of resemblance" and "likeness" associated with mimetic realism (154–55).

4   It is worth noting here that the 1982 production starring Griffiths was co-authored by Campbell, unlike the 1986 version, but the critical emphasis on visibility politics failed to notice the more marginal role that Campbell played in the development of the later play starring Indigenous women.

subordinate clause indicating that *Jessica* was based on Campbell's life or her autobiography *Halfbreed*, or that it was written in collaboration with Campbell, is enough to secure the widespread interpretation of the play as a faithful and truthful account of her life experiences. This scant critical attention to Campbell's role in the making of *Jessica* mirrors her subordinate and subordinated status as Griffiths's collaborator. The majority of reviews, however, do not even mention *Jessica* was "written in collaboration with Maria Campbell," constructing Griffiths as the sole author of the play by giving her exclusive credit for the work. This not only betrays a lack of cultural sensitivity in the mainstream press to the question of who has the right or *authori*ty to tell Indigenous stories, it also doubly erases and marginalizes Campbell from a theatrical representation that was originally intended to facilitate her own cultural self-expression. She becomes an absented presence in this critical discourse. The simple fact that the play was based on Campbell's life serves as the ground upon which truth claims are made, and yet she remains for the most part unnamed and uncelebrated as a co-creator of the play. She is part of the authenticating discourse that constructs *Jessica* as a site of Indigenous representation while also taking a back seat to Griffiths, the white playwright whose work is celebrated as an individual achievement by a critical discourse that frequently fails to acknowledge the cross-cultural collaboration.

The critical tendency to overlook not only the play's authorship but also Campbell's peripheral role as Griffiths's collaborator reveals a lack of sensitivity to the question of who speaks for whom that would later galvanize political discussions of cultural appropriation in the late 1980s and early 1990s. Just as the casting of *Jessica* met the new political agenda of the 1980s with its focus on increased visibility, *The Book of Jessica* was published during an important turning point in history when concepts of cultural appropriation entered into mainstream critical and theoretical debates. In 1988, the Women's Press published new guidelines that mandated against works by white authors written from the perspective of non-white cultures. This move proved highly controversial, prompting the resignation of one of the editors for the press and sparking many heated debates within the Writers' Union and feminist publications such as *Broadside* (Stasiulis 39). Critical response was divided between those who defended freedom of the imagination and declared themselves "anti-censorship" and those who supported the right of Indigenous writers and writers of colour to tell their own stories (39–40). Moreover, as Michael Jacklin notes, Lee Maracle's "Moving Over" was published "the same year as *The Book of Jessica* and Lenore Keeshig-Tobias's 'Stop Stealing Native Stories' appeared next.[5] The following year, 'Whose Voice is it Anyway' established the discussion as central to the Canada Council and critical to contemporary Canadian cultural production" (124). This led to discussions in *The Globe and Mail*, arguing "that grants should not be given to writers who wrote about cultures other than their own, unless they collaborated with people of that culture" (124).

Written in 1989, *The Book of Jessica* was, therefore, at the vanguard of a new political moment and movement that raised important questions about voice, authorship, representation, and identity. Though written to expose the cultural appropriation that took place behind the scenes of *Jessica*, the book was soon criticized for ironically perpetuating and reproducing the very relations of power it set out to critique. Despite the dialogic construction of the text, which gives voice to both Griffiths's and Campbell's views on the making of *Jessica*, Helen Hoy argues that Griffiths continued to exert white authorial power and editorial control over this material because she arranged and selected it for publication, put her name first in analphabetic order before Campbell's, and provided a framing structure in the form of both a third-person and first-person narrator. In addition, she sets Campbell's dialogue apart from the main narrative in smaller size font. However, Hoy fails to note that Griffiths dispenses with the narrative frame and gives both voices equal space and font size in "The Red Cloth," the second section of the dialogic introduction. Indeed, as David Jefferess points out, Campbell arguably dominates this part of the narrative, since her "voice begins [each of the] sub-sections" and thereby "initiates their content," even though "it may be

---

5   In an interview cited in Jacklin's article, Griffiths reveals that "Lenore Keeshig-Tobias phoned [her] and said, 'Thank you for your offering.'" Griffiths goes on to explain that she was deeply moved and honoured to hear this from "one of the toughest political people at that time, very vocal and public when she felt there was appropriation" (129).

presumed that [Griffiths] constructed these excerpts of dialogue and created their headings" (227). Interestingly, Hoy also concedes that Campbell powerfully resists and disrupts Griffiths's controlling discourse at every turn, leading to an open, though conflicted, dialogue of "*mutual* disputation/negotiation." "What could be static documentation is repeatedly problematized and transformed," according to Hoy, "through the dynamic of instant accountability, correction and challenge" (31; emphasis in original).

Following Hoy's lead, critics such as Kathleen Venema, Jennifer Andrews, and Susanna Egan see Griffiths's voice in *The Book of Jessica* as dominant and privileged due to her roles as both a speaking subject *and* the authoritative narrator, while Campbell is cast as the "resister to Griffiths' story" (Jefferess 221).[6] By celebrating Campbell's critical interventions, these studies view the dialogic text as a productive site for exposing the clash of cultures, perspectives, and subject positions between the two collaborators, who find themselves separated by the barriers of age, race, class, culture, language, and nation. This opens up for consideration the many ways in which white settler ideologies of colonialism and bourgeois individualism conflict with Indigenous cultural values and perspectives.[7] By revealing these contradictory values,

---

6   For instance, Venema argues Griffiths's "enormously appropriative" narrative "was critically and fundamentally disrupted by Maria Campbell, the uniquely, inimitably, and persistently *present* 'othered subject'" (35); Egan likewise claims "the text . . . reasserts a Native voice in a situation we might commonly describe as appropriative" by introducing a "Native aesthetic," though she takes a more optimistic view, arguing that this aspect of the text "challenges boundaries as boundaries, transforming the conflictual binaries of the original situation into a continuous . . . healing circle" (12, 10).

7   These issues, which have been discussed extensively in the scholarship on *The Book of Jessica*, include the text's discussion of "the red cloth" as part of an Indigenous gift economy versus the acts of theft and appropriation attributed to an imperialist ideology of conquest (Murray); the Indigenous focus on community versus white bourgeois individualism; the Indigenous notion of shared ownership versus a Lockean notion of individual ownership and property rights; the oral and dynamic nature of Indigenous storytelling versus the Eurocentric privileging of the written word (Chester and Dudoward; Boardman); the Indigenous value of listening and sharing as an antidote to colonial relations of appropriation (Egan).

together with the messy personal conflicts and artistic negotiations that led to the making of *Jessica*, the text's performative dialogue of competing voices constructs meaning and subjectivity as plural, heterogeneous, and unstable. Nevertheless, much of the early criticism of *The Book of Jessica* insists that Griffiths's control over the making of the dialogic narrative problematically reinforces the relations of power and privilege that created the unequal theatrical exchange in the first place. These studies also critique the ways in which Griffiths reproduces colonialist attitudes and assumptions,[8] and replays "conventional Eurocentric responses of nostalgia, romance, or guilt" (Egan 16).

Though such scholarship has carefully examined how *The Book of Jessica* both challenges and perpetuates colonialist ideologies and relations of power, Lorraine York believes that critical discussions of the text's dialogic form often "replicate the property dispute that lies at the heart of [the] text: the theft of stories by white artists" (174). By arguing, in effect, "that out of the collaborative venture a single author emerges to exert control," critics such as Hoy, Venema, Andrews, and Egan condemn Griffiths for taking ownership of the text away from Campbell, yet they also attempt to "relocate authorial control," and by extension ownership, to Campbell by examining her acts of post-colonial resistance (171, 174).[9] This critical balancing act continuously repeats and rehearses the problem of appropriation, refusing to view the text as a shared, albeit conflicted, site of cross-cultural collaboration. "It

---

8   As many critics note, Griffiths draws on numerous stereotypical analogies, such as homesteading, the imperialist plundering of riches (in her image of the treasure chest), "the racist colonial dying native trope" (Forsyth 29), and the white anthropological fascination with native rituals and ceremony (as noted in Griffiths's reference to the Sundance photograph and in her description of the ceremony she attended, which blatantly disrespects Campbell's insistence that it is taboo to share this information publicly). Interestingly, Hoy observes that "the text seems concocted to provide the full panoply of colonial assumptions" (29), and Griffiths more or less confirms this point in her interview with Jacklin, when she says, "I deliberately included, even created parts that made me look bad" (129).

9   Like Jefferess, York also includes Jeanne Perreault's article as an example of a critic who attributes ownership of the text to Griffiths. However, both York and Jefferess argue that Perreault's study differs from the others because she does not view Campbell solely as a resistant other.

may be that the assumption that collaboration is going to be a meeting of equals appears to be so patently contradicted by appropriative aspects of this text," according to York, "that critics have difficulty regarding it as a collaboration at all, or else they suspect that to view it as one would be to make a claim for some sort of basic egalitarianism in the text" (174–75). However, by theorizing "collaboration as a sometimes uneasy negotiation of undeniable power functions," York reads *The Book of Jessica* as "a collaboration in which both authors participated, to some degree, in a utopian vision of what collaboration would effect, only to have that idealism harshly corrected by the power and pain that can be unleashed in a cross-cultural collaboration in a country haunted by imperialism" (175). Similarly, Jefferess argues that traditional "conceptions of collaboration limit the practice to an act performed by those who are 'equal' and like-minded," but *The Book of Jessica* "challenges . . . such narrow constructions" (223). "The conversations in *The Book of Jessica*," instead, "reveal a collaborative interdependence or intimate connection that is marked by difference rather than harmony; their collaboration reveals the interdependence of subjects within a structure of unequal power rather than a 'merging' of individual subjectivities" (234).

By arguing that collaborative writing needs to be understood as a contested site of meaning between two subjects who are not always equal, rather than as a merging of selves, York and Jefferess refute the initial reception of *The Book of Jessica* as a final act of ownership and control by a white author. They also recuperate Campbell's agency and role in the creation of *The Book of Jessica* by acknowledging her shared authorship of a text that is nevertheless conflicted by relationships of power and difference. This, in turn, opens up a reading of *The Book of Jessica* as a cross-cultural middle ground of representation. As Jefferess argues, viewing the text within "a single author-paradigm" that privileges Griffiths's subjectivity sets up a binary opposition between "a dominant Linda and an exploited Maria," locking Campbell in the role of "the resistant 'other' to the *authori*tative Linda" (226; emphasis in original). Drawing on Homi K. Bhabha's belief that "[c]olonial relations of power . . . are never as straightforward and one-way as the coloniser/colonised construction" (235), Jefferess claims the conversations in *The Book of Jessica* reveal the "ever shifting, tense and ambivalent relations of power between the two authors" (221). Though he does not deny the many differences and inequalities between the two women, his interpretation of the text as a site of post-colonial ambivalence rejects the critical tendency to view their relationship in exclusively binary terms.

Richard J. Lane takes a similar, though more optimistic, view, reading *The Book of Jessica* as a "third space" of transcultural communication that "go[es] beyond centered, hierarchical relations of power, being, and knowledge" (153). Jessie Forsyth likewise examines moments of "intersubjective struggle" in the book as a "potentially transformative, if painful, process" that gestures toward a shared space of understanding, though she warns this does not take away from the many conflicts and tensions between the two women (57). Similarly, York picks up on Egan's claim that "'the relationship between the two women in the text refuses the oppositional and works instead toward a mutual recognition,'" adding, "[i]t may be more accurate to say that the text engages the oppositional and thus works toward a mutual recognition that is, I think, posited as a horizon but never reached" (177). While these readings view *The Book of Jessica* as provisional and open-ended, a site of struggle and transformation, they caution against a utopian reading, since the relations of power and inequality explored in the text are never resolved.

York's—as well as Jefferess's—view of cross-cultural collaboration as a shared but conflicted process of creation that takes place within unequal power structures provides a useful framework for looking back once more at the production and reception of *Jessica*. Rather than view the 1986 version of the play as the exclusive work of the "author" Linda Griffiths, which York attributes to the critical tendency to privilege "institutional markers of ownership," this alternative theory of collaboration opens up a space for acknowledging the many subjects who created *Jessica*, despite the hierarchies and inequities that shaped the play's process of development (172). When Campbell approached Thompson to help her write a play based on her life—agreeing to work with him, Griffiths, and a cast of white and Indigenous actors—their collaboration was an important meeting ground for white and Indigenous artists. However, as *The Book of Jessica* explains, this theatrical exchange was marked by unequal power relations that Campbell views in terms of a colonialist legacy of trade, conquest, and broken treaties. First and foremost, the white members of the collective, the director Thompson and star actor Griffiths, were in positions of dominance, replicating colonialist relations of power between white settler and Indigenous cultures. In addition to the fact that "the process" relied on their theatrical "expertise and specialization," derived from Thompson's methods of collective creation (Boardman 29), the institutional and cultural context in which the play was produced also privileged the white participants. Thompson was a leading figure of the alternative theatre movement of the 1970s, developing his unique form of collective creation in response to the cultural need at that time for stories to mythologize the Canadian nation.[10] This ideological and institutional context proved problematic to Campbell, whose novel *Halfbreed* was part of an Indigenous "counter discourse against the Canadian state" that exposed colonialist violence and oppression, challenging notions of cultural and national unity (Saul 145). As Joanne Saul argues, Thompson's "strong sense of nationalism" therefore "conflicts with Campbell's self-positioning as a mixed-race woman with an ambivalent relationship to 'Canada,' whose identity itself is a negotiation between (at least) two cultures" (141–42).

Despite the political and cultural conflicts caused by the unequal relations of power that shaped this theatrical exchange, *Jessica* does reflect Campbell's ambivalent notion of personal and national identity, most notably through the mixed-race ceremony and clash of cultures depicted in its theatrical narrative. The play also, arguably, met Campbell's initial goal of giving back to her people when it was produced in Saskatoon. As Campbell notes repeatedly in *The Book of Jessica*, she views art as a form of "community work" that is socially accountable (69). "Real art," she explains, "gives . . . back to you and heals you, empowers you, and it's beautiful" (83). Since the original production was performed for mixed audiences, including her own local Métis and

---

10   Though the play eventually moved from the realm of collective creation to become a co-authored piece, it was nevertheless a product of Thompson's process and 25th Street Theatre in Saskatoon, an institution that was linked to Thompson and Theatre Passe Muraille in Toronto, one of the founding alternative theatres in Canada.

Indigenous communities, it was closer to Campbell's social, political, and artistic vision than the 1986 productions in Ontario and Quebec that removed the play from the local community for which it was originally intended. The earlier version of *Jessica* thus occupied an important middle ground that brought together Indigenous and white actors and audiences for a play that was celebrated for spreading a positive message of hope. Unlike the tragic ending of Ryga's *The Ecstasy of Rita Joe*, which depicts the main character as a powerless victim of colonial sexual violence, *Jessica* concludes, triumphantly, with "'a power song' of recognition and healing" (Debenham 147). Taking place within a traditional ceremony that connects the act of naming with the sounds of giving birth, this final image symbolizes both a personal and cultural rebirth for the protagonist.

This empowering message—key to both versions of *Jessica*—reflects Campbell's vision of art as a form of cultural healing and, therefore, suggests that her role in the creation of the play was important to the ongoing redefinition of theatrical narratives of Indigeneity in the 1980s. Tantoo Cardinal also contributed to the text's depiction of Indigenous cultures as a member of the original collective. According to *The Book of Jessica*, "Tantoo worked on a character based on her grandmother" that would later serve as the basis for Vitaline. Moreover, "[i]t was through this old lady of Tantoo's that [Griffiths] began to understand Native humour" (41). The reader also learns that Campbell asked Cardinal to teach Griffiths how to chant in order to sing Jessica's power song at the end of the play (52). These examples of Cardinal's active role in the early development of *Jessica* suggest that the theatrical text bears the traces of her personal, artistic, and cultural contributions, which were shared orally and performatively (in keeping with Indigenous traditions of knowledge transmission).[11] Unlike the critical discourse of visibility politics that viewed Cardinal's performance as an essentialist reflection of

---

11   It should be noted that this process of collaborative oral exchange is also a feature of Thompson's theatrical methodology. This may explain why his approach to collective creation appealed to Campbell, since it seemed to "fit with the oral, communal nature of [Indigenous] storytelling" (Debenham 145).

an embodied truth, *The Book of Jessica* thus credits her as a collaborator and co-creator of the play.

As Campbell explains in *The Book of Jessica,* the play does not belong exclusively to Griffiths or Campbell:

> But in *Jessica*, who created the story? I didn't create it myself and you didn't either. We have to stop thinking "you and me." There were other people in the room whose energy, yes, even words, went into creating it, and here we are spreading our wings and saying, "Mine." That's what people do with lands when they fight over them . . . (91)

By acknowledging the many voices that went into the making of *Jessica*, Campbell dismantles the primacy of the "author," itself the product of white bourgeois ideology and institutions, in favour of a collective model consistent with Indigenous views of art as cultural rather than individual property. This cultural perspective likewise constructs the play as shared ground rather than territory to be claimed by imperialist ideology. Despite the fact that Griffiths would later take over "authorship" of *Jessica*, in a problematic replay of colonialist relations of power and appropriation, Campbell's emphasis on the multiple subjects who created *Jessica* acknowledges the collaborative, though highly conflicted, theatrical process that took place behind the scenes. While the shared meeting ground that gave birth to *Jessica* was not a utopian space free of colonialist relations, it was nevertheless the product of a collaborative exchange between white and Indigenous participants. The resulting play covered new representational ground, leading to the first professional theatrical production in Canada about a Métis woman's life experiences that included Indigenous women's acting and writing contributions.

In this sense, we can view *Jessica* as an important transitional play, occupying a cross-cultural middle ground that linked Indigenous and white theatre artists prior to the establishment of professional Indigenous theatres in Canada. Due to the lack of such institutions in the period leading up to the first production of *Jessica* in 1982, Campbell made the difficult decision to collaborate with a white-dominated theatre in order to have her work produced professionally. This changed in 1986 when Native Earth Performing Arts became the first professional Indigenous theatre in Canada, quickly reaching national acclaim with its production of Tomson Highway's *The Rez Sisters* that same year. Thanks to the success of Native Earth Performing Arts and other identity-based theatres formed in the 1980s, such as Buddies in Bad Times Theatre and Nightwood Theatre, this historical development led to the second wave of theatre in Canada. The rise of these new theatre companies challenged the nationalist discourse of the 1970s by drawing attention to differences such as gender, race, ethnicity, and sexuality. Begun as a collective creation under the direction of alternative theatre icon Paul Thompson, *Jessica* stood on the cusp of these two movements. It was originally a product of the alternative theatre, yet it moved dramatic representation in Canada toward a new identity politics devoted to questions of gender and race.

The network of actors that created *Jessica* also linked these two theatrical traditions. Two of the Indigenous women cast in the 1986 production, Monique Mojica and Makka Kleist, were instrumental in the formation of Native Earth Performing Arts (NEPA), which they joined during its early amateur phase in 1983. As members of NEPA, they would go on to perform in Highway's *The Rez Sisters* shortly after the successful run of *Jessica*. Cardinal and Greene, who were a part of the original *Jessica* collective, quickly became two of the most successful Indigenous actors of their generation, starring in countless plays and films in Canada and Hollywood. In an interview with Jacklin, Griffiths comments that *Jessica* "was the beginning of a connection between my theatre community, especially at Theatre Passe Muraille, and the Native world" (130). The play was thus an important, albeit highly conflicted, meeting ground for these two theatre communities: an intermediate step toward the sweeping changes that would later transform theatre in Canada during the period between the production of *Jessica* in 1986 and the publication of *The Book of Jessica* in 1989.

Native Earth Performing Arts effectively ushered in a new era of theatrical representation in Canada, following the success of Highway's *The Rez Sisters* in 1986. According to the company's mandate, it "provided a base for professional Native performers, writers, technicians, and other artists" (qtd.

in Preston 140). Beginning in 1988, NEPA would nurture a new generation
of Indigenous playwrights with the Weesageechak Begins to Dance festival, which continues to this day. Together with the public outcry against the
appropriation of voice in literary and academic debates of the late 1980s, this
new development in Canadian theatre called for Indigenous theatre artists to
write, perform, and produce their own stories on the professional stage. From
this point forward, a new political discourse was increasingly supported by
mainstream culture, enabling Indigenous theatre artists to "tak[e] back [their]
right to speak," as Yvette Nolan puts it (qtd. in Carter 178). This served as
a marked contrast to the period between 1982 and 1986, when the critical
reception of *Jessica* in the mainstream press focused exclusively on the visual
field as a site for considering the question of cultural identity and theatrical
representation without pausing to consider the complex question of the play's
authorship and the institutional context that produced it.

When *The Book of Jessica* was published in 1989, its discussion of voice
appropriation contributed to this new social and political transformation of
theatrical discourses in Canada that supported the right to self-representation for Indigenous theatre artists. By exposing the relations of power and
difference that led to the making of *Jessica* just a few years earlier, *The Book
of Jessica* was one of the first texts to openly discuss the issue of cultural
appropriation in the Canadian theatre while also raising questions about the
problems of cross-cultural collaboration in an unequal society. While many
scholars have critiqued the book for reinscribing the hierarchies of power it
set out to critique, the strength of the dialogic narrative lies not in its ability
to neutralize or resolve these differences, but to put them on view for the first
time. As Joanne Tompkins argues, building on Griffiths's observation in *The
Book of Jessica* that it is "'the story of the rehearsals [that] never ends,'" the
text ultimately resists closure: "There is always a 'post'-script in which more
is rehearsed. The relationship, the play, and the white / Metis / native dia-
logues will have to continue to be negotiated, rehearsed, and replayed" (39).
This, in turn, implies that social change in the theatre—and by extension the
political arena—is an ongoing and never-ending process of transformation
that requires open dialogue.

In an interesting turn of events that speaks to this ongoing process of political and cultural renegotiations in the theatre, one of Griffiths's solo plays was recently restaged—and re-"appropriated"—by a Métis director and a Colombian-born performer. When *Alien Creature: a visitation from Gwendolyn MacEwen* was remounted at Theatre Passe Muraille in 2017, on the same stage where Griffiths originally performed the play in 1999, Beatriz Pizano captivated critics and audiences with her powerful performance. In a talkback session for the show, she explained that she chose to play the part with her own Colombian accent rather than imitate a Canadian one in order to challenge audience expectations by normalizing this ostensible sign of "difference" (Lauzon and Pizano). She also claimed she felt accepted as "Canadian" for the first time when she was cast in the role of an iconic Canadian poet written by a famous Canadian playwright. While this comment reveals that discrimination in the theatre is still unfortunately a reality today, it also tells us that taking ownership of Griffiths's play and embodying an Anglo-Canadian poet, who is in many ways a stand-in for the playwright herself, was a political act for Pizano—a turning point in her career that transformed her sense of cultural, national, and artistic identity. In Jani Lauzon's commentary, she reinterpreted the play from an Indigenous perspective, likening the motif of the circle in *Alien Creature* to Indigenous cultural imagery (which also, interestingly, recalls the ceremonial circle in *Jessica*). This cross-cultural reinvention of a work by Linda Griffiths that challenges white normativity, through the collaborative partnership of a Métis director and a Latin Canadian performer, points to yet another political and social intervention into mainstream theatre in Canada. By raising important questions about the underlying relations of power that shape theatrical representations, *The Book of Jessica* provides us with a useful model for exploring these changes while resisting easy or ready-made resolutions, suggesting that this process is complex, ongoing, and open to change, the result of political and cultural struggles that continue to transform and challenge the way theatre in Canada is produced and understood.

GAME DEVELOPMENT: LINDA GRIFFITHS'S *GAMES: WHO WANTS TO PLAY?*

SHELLEY SCOTT

In this essay, I will trace the development process behind Linda Griffiths's play *Games: Who Wants to Play?*, which was published in 2016. My first encounter with the work was in 2011 when Griffiths visited the University of Lethbridge with a script called *Games to be Played with Caution*. Drawing on interviews with participants, I will describe the development project that took place in Lethbridge and then explore the changes that occurred between the earlier versions and the production at Alberta Theatre Projects in Calgary in 2014. Finally, I will consider the play within the thematic context of Griffiths's career, showing how it develops her fascination with fantasy, group identity, and belonging. The play features another in Griffiths's series of complex female characters but, uniquely, the woman in question is the mother of a troubled teenage boy, and *Games: Who Wants to Play?* gives Griffiths an opportunity to engage with youth culture to an unusual and profound degree.

Because this project marks one of the last that Griffiths was able to complete, and because it incorporates so many of the techniques for which she was known—from devising and using her visceral playwriting method with students, to producing at Alberta Theatre Projects with a strong creative team, to exploring female subjectivity—the process behind *Games: Who Wants to Play?* is a rich opportunity to appreciate Griffiths's contribution to Canadian theatre one more time. Griffiths's recurring themes are explored through an immersion in contemporary youth culture. While Griffiths herself was, sadly, at the end of her career, her final play gave her the opportunity to return to the concerns of youth, to explore the alien world of a teenaged protagonist, and to delve into a culture of gaming she knew little about.

GAME OVER

From September 12 to 24 of 2011, Linda Griffiths spent two weeks as a visiting artist at the University of Lethbridge, working with students enrolled in instructor Gail Hanrahan's Canadian Plays in Development course. Griffiths brought a new two-act play, called *Games to be Played With Caution*, which the students first encountered with a read-through. The play has five roles (two female, three male), so the fourteen students took turns reading the parts. Griffiths was mainly interested in researching the experiences and attitudes of young people toward online gaming, a generation and a world with which she had little connection. She asked the students to come to class having interviewed someone about their relationship to gaming. The students returned and performed their characters—friends, relatives, or strangers—and from that material Griffiths began to shape what would become a brand new theatre piece, called *Game Over*.

One of the students, Lauren Hyatt,[1] explained:

> [S]he wanted us to gather real stories. Ones that related to sexuality, pornography, video games—basically any theme contained within the play we read. We were then tasked with recreating these stories keeping as true to the person's use of physicality, language—in fact trying to keep it word for word. From these stories we chose a few scenes to incorporate into the final product that came out of this class: a physical, collectively-created cacophony based around first person shooter games and the famous role playing game: World of Warcraft.[2]

---

1   At the time of the course the student's name was Lauren Steyn.

2   "World Of Warcraft is a Massively Multiplayer Online Role Playing Game with millions of players and was released in 2004. The game features players interacting with each other within a fantasy world via avatars. Players are encouraged to cooperate and compete with each other. Player progression is measured through multiple levels which are determined by the accumulation of experience points and items which increase the characters' power. Wealth is measured through the accumulation of in-game currency which includes gold, silver, and copper pieces. [. . . Literature] likens the evolution and development of WOW

What emerged was a show separate from, but parallel to, *Games to be Played with Caution*. Student participant Erica Barr noted that the class never returned to the original script after the initial read-through, and Griffiths was far more interested in what the students created. Barr commented that the reaction of students, both participants and spectators, was one of tremendous excitement, as they saw a topic being addressed that they felt was relevant to their lives and their generation. Some of the people who had been interviewed by the students attended the performance, and again were impressed with theatre that spoke to their own interests. Student Cameron Lomon recalled: "I remember a lot of students being excited, because it was not something they had seen. They had not seen devised theatre or a show about themselves before." Erica Barr observed that the young woman she interviewed "thought it was so cool that it was something she knew about." Barr commented that audiences really enjoyed "that it was a weird live action fantasy raid" and contained references to "things kids our age all know and think are funny."

Lomon further recalled two things that struck him most vividly about Griffiths's working method. First, she would always direct the students to "come in full," meaning to come into the class period with raw material they were ready to work on, to be fully present and engaged. Second, Lomon noticed how observant Griffiths was, how she herself was always interested and responsive to what the students did, and how she would always pick up on some detail to develop further. As Barr concluded, "I felt like I had a lot of ownership over the final performance." Participant Sean Guist observed that online games are a kind of parallel universe to reality, and that the class creation, *Game Over*, was a kind of parallel universe to Griffiths's play. The students took ideas, themes, and emotions from the reading of the play and created new scenes, with no expectation that they would return to the script (Guist).

Playwright Meg Braem had her play *Exia* developed by the same class later in the semester, and she was present for Griffiths's visit. Braem agrees that Griffiths's method was not a traditional form of dramaturgy, but rather

---

to be a parallel civilization, if not for the population but for the social environment where millions of players interact within" (Ford 4).

that she used her play as a "jumping-off point." Braem points out that *Game Over* was all student-generated work, describing it as a "cabaret surrounding this idea" of online gaming and noting that Griffiths would "illuminate" the connections between student-generated ideas. Braem observed that Griffiths was accustomed to leading a group and was very comfortable with the process, and that she was genuinely interested in everything everyone had to offer.

Griffiths had been offering workshops for some time in what she called "Visceral Playwriting," encounters of various lengths, sometimes just pure process, sometimes with a final presentation. The experience could be as short as two to four hours, or as long as two months. Lauren Hyatt recalls: "Linda introduced us to the 'The Jam' [. . .] It was sort of getting sound and action into our body: we used our bodies as instruments to discover where our impulses were and to follow them. It was an awesome way to put any discussion we had had into practice." As a graduate student and teaching assistant, Sean Guist took on the role of recorder and note-keeper, recalling:

> The exercises we used were all thematic explorations of her play: coming of age; gaming; technology; global impact; passage of male adolescence; parallel universes [. . .]. Linda started paring [the material] down and picking out moments and images and ideas. From there, she encouraged the actors to learn the language of their characters as this could lead to "germs of possibility," and to think about how to create a game with combat and characters. We then kept working and shuffling scenes, fine-tuning motifs and ideas. We came up with twelve scenes with gaming transitions, and created a map of the progression, order, actors, transitions and key phrases that had to be kept.

Griffiths did some directing in rehearsals too, mainly to guide audience focus. It was a quick process: for example, in the rehearsal I observed, one student mentioned an anecdote from his own life at the start of the session, and from that came three scenes about relationships. Griffiths clarified that, in a real production circumstance, they would be careful not to use the verbatim story, and would make a composite character instead, but that within the creative rehearsal process they are "amoral" about stealing material (personal interview). Sean Guist explains: "She spoke about 'visceral playwriting' and that it was about emotions/feelings/actions/experience rather than plot, and often was explored through personal experiences and reflections and interviews and that all jumping off points are worth exploring [. . .] My notes have Linda saying 'GO FOR IT EMOTIONALLY' and for each performer to choose a specific narrative line for their character and to then find allies amongst other narrative lines" (emphasis in original).

In my conversation with instructor Gail Hanrahan and students Cameron Lomon and Erica Barr, the consensus was that Griffiths was encountering a subject matter and dealing with an age group that, as Barr described it, was "really foreign to her." Lomon observed that Griffiths "was excited about how ignorant she was," and excited to talk to people who were a part of a different world. The students introduced her to the reality of "how obsessive kids can get; they have no social lives except online" (Barr). Hanrahan agreed that Griffiths was interested in the age group of the students: "She knew she didn't know this world, the game but also youth. She wanted to explore what the games meant and how people that age talk about them. She was going out on a limb with something she knew nothing about."

At the final performance, Griffiths commented that, if she were to continue to work on *Game Over* as a separate entity, she would investigate gender further, go back to the beginning of the process, and get the students to do more interviews and research. She concluded that there was no "message" to *Game Over*, that there was no attempt to be balanced or comprehensive in the treatment of gaming, but rather that the work offered these specific actors' take on it. Interestingly, Griffiths also commented that she found the students more judgmental of gaming than she was herself; she compared video games favourably to her own escape into literature as a child (personal interview).

GAMES TO BE PLAYED WITH CAUTION

Griffiths's work on *Game Over* with students at the University of Lethbridge provided her with unique first-hand accounts of online gaming culture that proved useful to the development of her manuscript, *Games to be Played with Caution*. Griffiths's script went on to a multi-staged development process, including a reading at the Banff Playwrights Colony, before premiering at the Alberta Theatre Projects's Enbridge playRites Festival from March 7 to April 5, 2014, with the title *Games: Who Wants to Play?*[3] It was the last playRites Festival mounted by ATP, and one of the last productions of a new play by Griffiths, who passed away later that year. In 2016, the play was published by Playwrights Canada Press, again entitled *Games: Who Wants to Play?*

The earlier play, *Games to Be Played with Caution*, exists in multiple versions, but to illustrate some of the development that took place I will refer here to the iteration from 2010 to demonstrate the evolving tactics Griffiths explored in order to represent the male adolescent obsession with gaming in youth culture. In the 2010 version, the play takes place in two time periods, starting with the present when a teenager, Zach, has been incarcerated in a psychiatric facility and is visited by his friend Micky in order to film a segment of their online game review series. The action then shifts to a time three years in the past (identified as the year 2008), where a multi-level set represents the upstairs adult world of Zach's parents, Dan and Marion, and the downstairs-level basement where Zach (age fifteen) and Micky (age sixteen) play games. In the ending of this version, Zach kills his parents by setting fire to their bed, thus explaining his incarceration in the present time period. Micky remains Zach's friend, visiting him even after the murder, so that the conflict in the play's world is clearly one of generational breakdown. Zach and Micky explicitly reject the adults' generation, saying, "They may never get it," meaning that they may never understand the appeal of youth culture,

3   I would like to thank Jamie Dunsdon, Amy Lynn Strilchuk, Vanessa Porteous, and Dianne Goodman for their research assistance. Many thanks as well to all the interview participants quoted in this paper.

particularly gaming; they characterize Zach's parents as aliens or zombies (*Games to be Played* 11).

This generational divide is related to various discussions around the importance of loyalty. In the 2010 version, Micky wants to replace the "clan" of online gamers he and Zach have been playing with, arguing, "We can't get anywhere with those guys, they're losers" (13). The boys' goal is to advance to higher levels and eventually become professional players like their idol Fakesharp99, who makes a lot of money by competing in tournaments (14). However, Zach rejects the notion of abandoning their team, feeling it would be a betrayal. Zach points out: "This is the kind of shit my Dad does, your Dad too. They tell them to fire people and they just do it" (14). However, Micky is less interested in concepts of honour, and he criticizes Zach's interest in myth-ological/fantasy world games where players co-operate, preferring instead the combat narratives and first-person shooter games (20).

Zach remains distant and disturbed in all the play's versions I have read, but the biggest difference is the eventual target of his anger. In *Games to be Played with Caution*, Zach sets fire to his parents' bed. In the final (produced and published) iteration, *Games: Who Wants to Play?*, Zach instead turns on and viciously beats Micky into unconsciousness, perhaps to death, before going upstairs and joining his parents in their bed for comforting "cuddles," like he did when he was a small child. His mother, Marion, has commented earlier that, while her generation rebelled against older people and the "estab-lishment" (she references the kidnapping perpetrated by the FLQ), she is confused by what she sees as her son's generation turning on their own. She cites infamous school shootings like the one in Columbine, where adolescents kill others of their own age (*Games: Who Wants to Play?* 72). Zach's attack on Micky would seem to be consistent with her observations, since he has chosen to take out his rage on a peer rather than his parents. Zach's violence toward Micky could even be seen as a rejection of his gaming addiction.

However, there are two complicating factors: first, Zach has filmed the attack on Micky and put it online in order for it to go "viral." In this sense, it is Zach's ultimate sign of commitment to a world in which only what happens online really matters. Second, as we in the audience see Zach get into bed with his parents—ostensibly a happy family ending—the body of Micky is still present in the downstairs world; it is only a matter of time before morning comes and the parents discover what their son has done. In this way, Zach has, perhaps more perversely than in the earlier draft, declared his total alliance with his peers and ruined his parents' lives.

In my conversation with Griffiths, she mentioned that the initial idea for *Games to be Played with Caution* was sparked by friends whose son became a professional poker player; she was fascinated with the idea of gaming for a living (personal interview).[4] In the "Playwright's Note" for the ATP production, Griffiths makes the subject matter more personal by relating the play to her brother. She writes that when she was nineteen and her brother was twelve,

> I watched my brother and his friend [. . .] go into the basement and basically not come out for five years. Then, after five years, I watched my brother emerge from the basement as a young man. What had happened? [. . .] It appeared that my brother had undergone a transformation more profound than the passage of time. When I began thinking of it later, it seemed a perilous journey for a boy to grow up [. . .] A passage between life and death. ("Playwright's Note: *Games*" 10).

In her note, Griffiths sympathizes with her friends who are mothers of troubled teenage boys. Despite coming from "great homes with smart and generous parents," these boys had difficulties that "seemed incomprehensible," including trouble getting through high school: "I began to be interested in the forces of male adolescence in the second decade of the two thousands. What was happening to the boys? That was the thread I followed over a trail of six years" ("Playwright's Note: *Games*" 10).[5]

---

4   Griffiths also confirmed that she was interested in pursuing a topic that was contemporary and male as a contrast to her previous play, *Age of Arousal* (personal interview).

5   Griffiths was tapping into a common fear in public discourse regarding teenage males. See Wente for one example.

According to ATP's production dramaturg Vicki Stroich, there was a strong team assisting Griffiths throughout the rewriting and rehearsal process, including dramaturg Daniel MacIvor and director Amiel Gladstone.[6] Stroich explains that they did not want an ending that was as "bleak" as Zach killing his parents: "There was a lot of discussion about our sympathies for the characters and whether we should have any. We decided we didn't want that ending for them." At the same time, they did want Zach to act out with some sort of violence. By choosing to have him go up to the parents' room with a candle, the danger is present but there is still a question in the audience's mind: "Could they heal? Would they turn him in? Would they come together as a family? They need to somehow deal with having a dead or injured teenager in their basement" (Stroich).

Stroich reports that the path to that choice was ever-changing, and that the ending was confirmed in pre-production workshops before rehearsals began. This decision in turn led to the question of why Zach turns against and beats his only friend, Micky. Stroich suggests there is a sense of rivalry with Micky: Zach feels that he is not the son his parents want and he is alienated from their lifestyle, while Micky does want their life and manages to be accepted by Zach's parents. Further, Micky makes it clear to Zach that he is only hanging out with him because Zach is "safe," a plot thread that escalated through the workshop process as Micky became the antagonist. As for the ambiguity of the ending, Griffiths wanted the audience to be uncertain whether Micky is dead; certainly, the intention was that Micky suffers a "savage" beating, but the choice was made not to explicitly say anything about death and to leave the ending unclear (Stroich).

In reference to the new ending, director Amiel Gladstone recalls:

The first ending [. . .] that I read was close to what was on stage, although probably more annihilistic. There was a version [. . .] where Zach had a can of gasoline which he poured everywhere as he was

---

6   In her playwright's note, Griffiths states that Daniel MacIvor had been working with her for the past year and a half as a dramaturg.

going up to his parent's bed, the idea being he was going to set everything alight as fires raged outside. It played as too cartoony to the rest
of the production and didn't have the right kind of weight. Having
Micky lying in a heap, not moving, and Zach climbing into bed with
his parents felt more like the tone the show needs. Everyone safe, but
not at all safe, cozy for the moment as a tight family, but things were
about to end. The bed being an island, as an attempt at refuge, but
just as dangerous as "out there" depending who you were in bed with.

Actor and playwright Karen Hines participated in a reading of the play in
Calgary that took place just before rehearsals began, and reports that Griffiths
was very happy with it. Hines believes that Griffiths decided to change the
ending, not because she was afraid to deal with dark subjects, but because
she did not feel the play necessarily warranted an ending quite that dark; she
imagined people leaving the theatre after seeing Zach murder his parents, and
"[s]he didn't want to do that to an audience." Hines speculates that, because
Griffiths herself was so ill and vulnerable at the time, she needed to end her
play on a more helpful and healing note.

Fascinated by the connection between teenagers, gaming, and violence,
Griffiths drew on the tragic case of a real-life Canadian teenager to add further nuance to her final version of *Games: Who Wants to Play?* She created
Michael Ferguson, a character who does not appear in earlier versions of the
script, is discussed but never appears on stage, and is dead before the play
begins. Vicki Stroich explains that the character is based on the death in 2008
of a real teenage boy in Ontario who ran away from home when his parents
took away his Xbox and then died after falling from a tree.[7] In the first scene,
Marion makes reference to Michael Ferguson and, when her husband Dan
does not recognize the name, she says: "He's dead. Haven't you seen the news?
His body was found out where they've let everything go wild [. . .] He ran

---

7   Brandon Crisp died 13 October 2008. In February of 2014, Toronto's Young People's
Theatre produced a play based on the incident called *n00b*, written by Christopher Duthie.
It was also produced in March of 2014 in Calgary as part of the Y Stage Theatre Series at
Vertigo Theatre.

away from home. I don't know what happened after that. Nobody knows" (7). Throughout the play, various theories about his death are offered:

> **MARION:** That's why he ran away. They stopped him from playing games. He runs away. He walks out of town onto the highway. A van stops to give him a ride. There is a man in the van, two men, a man and a woman, a group of angry teenagers. Hikers find his body weeks later, in the gorge, naked, eaten by animals. (29)

In Act Two, as Micky and Dan bond over a beer, they theorize that Michael Ferguson "was into snuff films." Dan confirms: "I heard that. He got involved with those snuff people. He met them online" (58). Perhaps the most important reference to the character occurs in an exchange between Marion and Zach as they do laundry together:

> **MARION:** He was a troubled young man.
>
> **ZACH:** How do you know?
>
> **MARION:** His parents were on the news.
>
> **ZACH:** What do parents know?
>
> **MARION:** Parents know their children.
>
> **ZACH:** Yeah?
>
> **MARION:** Yeah.
>
> **ZACH:** When does that happen? (44–45)

After a pause, Marion responds by telling Zach about being pregnant with him and about his birth, implying that she wishes he was still that simple for his parents to "know." The play concludes with Zach telling an entirely innocent version of the Michael Ferguson story—that he had simply climbed up into a cave to read a book, tried to set a fire, and slipped and fell—concluding, "There was no evil" (78).

According to Vicki Stroich, what fascinated Griffiths was that the real boy's death was not a murder or the result of violence. While everyone "assumed the worst, it was actually pretty run of the mill. The boogeyman of teenage violence was actually remarkably innocent" (Stroich). In the play, the parents focus on their fear of the worst that could happen. According to Stroich, "Zach is not a burgeoning monster until his parents make him one [. . .] the parents are the manipulators." Stroich observes that Griffiths was concerned about "the way the world is for parents and teenagers," and came to see the parents as the problem: "they were building what Zach became by creating their vision of how things were going wrong."

Reviews of the 2014 ATP production uniformly picked up on this theme of the parents' manipulative game-playing. Ruth Myles states explicitly: "Everyone in the play is running some sort of game: Dan and Marion play at being a happily married couple, despite the fact their union is based on a lie." Myles is referring to Dan's revelation that he deliberately damaged a condom in order to get Marion pregnant when she was still reluctant to have children. Myles goes on to point out that Micky "plays up his role as the friend the parents like, with an eye to becoming part of the family." Here, Myles is noting Micky's deliberate appeal to Zach's parents, playing the young suitor to Marion and the best buddy to Dan. The reviewer also alludes to the new presence added to the script since its earlier versions: "And at the centre of it all is the death of Zach's friend Michael Ferguson. Was he kidnapped? Was he a troubled teen who ran away when his video games were taken away? Or was he just a boy who died in a tragic accident?" Myles finds the dialogue between the parents "stilted and forced," while the actors playing Zach and Micky "fare better, imbuing their teen talk with alternating doses of passion and disdain."

Louis Hobson, writing for the *Calgary Sun*, is more positive, calling the play "a topnotch drama that rips its heart from news headlines and any number of talk shows. Parents, educators and authorities are convinced that the violent, sadistic video games young people play these days are turning them into potential monsters." Like Myles, Hobson notes "that we realize that everyone in the house is playing some kind of game, some of which are really dangerous sexually, emotionally and intellectually." Hobson picks up on the ambiguity of Zach's motivations and links it to the mystery of what really happened to Michael Ferguson; his death "could be as innocent or malevolent as Zach might be which each audience member must determine on their own. [. . .] One moment I was convinced [Daniel] Maslany's Zach was a totally misunderstood innocent teen but then I watched those eyes when he confronted his parents and eventually [Richard] Lee Hsi [who played Micky]. There was something there beyond just a temper tantrum." Also, like Myles, Hobson finds the teenage characters believable but the adults stilted, and wonders if that was Griffiths's—and the actors'—intention. He concludes that "[p]sychological horror is a genre few playwrights dare tackle which makes Griffiths' invitation to join *Games: Who Wants to Play?* one not to dismiss too lightly," a quote used on the cover of the published text.

Finally, reviewer Jessica Goldman is the most positive of all in her assessment, and astutely picks up on Griffiths's intentions. Like the other reviewers, Goldman notices that "everyone is playing some kind of game" in the play and calls it "zeitgeisty," praising Griffiths's ambiguous ending because it "smartly leaves the audience asking questions without succumbing to the preachy tropes so often found around issue plays." Goldman lists the games being played: Marion plays at being the cool parent, but really wants Zach "to go back to being the sweet little boy she once knew"; Dan plays at being the disciplinarian when he really wants a friend to drink beer and play hockey with him; Micky plays at being confident "but he's ashamed of his immigrant family and is looking for surrogate parents to befriend."

Like the other reviewers, Goldman concludes that Zach is the character that interests Griffiths the most "as she explores the impact and possible dangers of gamer culture on a family." His parents are concerned but afraid to do anything about his gaming, and when they finally do, their action "launches Zach's behaviour in several different directions that at once confirm his parent's fears of the negative impact of gaming yet also shows that the only evil in gaming is people's fear of it." She asks if "video game violence is harming the boys or is it simply the new tribalism by which young men bond and establish themselves," suggesting that the kinds of games the parents play are far more potentially harmful. Goldman also cites Zach's sweet relationship with his virtual girlfriend Keira as evidence that he "is a good kid. But never far from our minds is the creepiness of the situation and Zach's obvious inability to socialize with any woman not of the virtual world." In her concluding recommendations, Goldman reiterates that "Griffiths isn't simply writing [games] off as unhealthy or dangerous. Instead she's asking questions about obsession and what it means to grow up well-adjusted in a world where gaming is the norm." Again returning to the theme of male adolescent rites of passage, she writes, "Young men have always found something to obsess about whether it was cars or music etc. and parents have always been worried about whether their son's passions were 'healthy'" (Goldman). Evidently, Goldman captured what Griffiths hoped to accomplish, for in an email to her director, Amiel Gladstone, Griffiths wrote, "That is a fabulous review. To know that someone on the outside understands is so huge—and for me to be called zeitgeitsy. What heaven" (qtd. in Gladstone).

GAMES: WHO WANTS TO PLAY?

As we have seen, the visceral playwriting technique that Griffiths developed, and her long experience with devising, served the University of Lethbridge students well as they explored the early version of her play. In turn, Griffiths took from them the first-hand experience of adolescents involved with gaming, their language and attitudes, and was able to develop her own script further until it was ready for production at ATP. The youth culture of role-playing and fantasy games like *World of Warcraft* posed a real fascination for Griffiths, which is not surprising for a writer known for adding some level of the mythological or fantastical to all her theatre creations. As Patricia Keeney writes: "Often referred to as her fabulist instinct and contextualized by her own production company, Duchess Productions, as a 'dance between the personal, the political, and the fantastic,' this non-naturalistic impulse (harnessed to real story) is her particular connection to the unknown, the unseen; it is her larger spiritual home" (iv). In an interview with Kathleen Gallagher, Griffiths acknowledges her commitment to a kind of spiritual dimension in each of her plays, observing, "[T]here are recurring themes in my work. There is almost always a point where somebody prays, for instance [. . .] you will find an element of the other dimension, fantasy, the fantastic" (Griffiths and Gallagher 120–21).

Griffiths has described her younger self as "a dreamy, floaty girl" ("Playwright Linda Griffiths"), recalling, "When I realized that fairy tales actually came out of a spiritual tradition, a shared mythological tradition which is also a psychological tradition, I finally stopped feeling ashamed. Because I had to stop myself back then, because I was really starting to live inside one of those books" (qtd. in Rudakoff 20). This is reminiscent of a comment she made to the students in Lethbridge, about being reluctant to play *World of Warcraft* herself because "it is so much up my alley" that she was afraid it would suck her in completely (personal interview). She clearly has empathy for the adolescent boys in *Games: Who Wants to Play?* They are deeply involved with their fantasy world, and once Zach is deprived of it, Griffiths understands that he acts out of a profound sense of loss.

In *Games: Who Wants to Play?*, Griffiths's abiding preoccupation with other, more mystical, realities thus finds expression in the alternative dimension of gaming. In an early interview with Judith Rudakoff, Griffiths talks about the many ways she relates to the idea of duality in her own personality (16). This play offers a strong example of this core theme of Griffiths's work, as it features a duality between adult culture and the teenagers' gaming culture, and forces of light and darkness are defined differently in the two worlds. The online character, Keira, for example, comes from the realm of Griffiths's beloved fairy tales, a beautiful and fragile girl who is loved by the young hero, Zach, who must save her from his own father. The father, Dan, becomes the villain in this fairy tale, casting an evil spell on Keira because his intentions for her are not pure: he desires Keira and uses her to spy on his son. Dan treats Keira like a pornographic program and then as spyware, while Keira and Zach define their relationship in terms of romantic, even poetic, love.

Consistent with her final play, *Games: Who Wants to Play?*, there are many examples in Griffiths's earlier plays where she incorporates the mystical and fantastical into the material; it can be seen as a through-line in her career. In the interview with Rudakoff, Griffiths describes how difficult it is to put into words the kinds of feelings and spiritual longing she wants to express, and she draws on the work of a feminist author to try to explain herself: "The American writer Starhawk has a good word, immanence, that she uses in *The Spiral Dance* and *Dreaming the Dark*. In using it she's trying to find a word to describe God that redefines it at the same time, that finds a new perspective on it. That's how I believe change, revolution, magic happens" (qtd. in Rudakoff 22). Starhawk writes from a radical/cultural feminism rooted in neo-paganism and goddess worship,[8] and a connection can be drawn to Griffiths's 1993 play *Spiral Woman and the Dirty Theatre*, in which she melds her spiritual quest with her experiences in the theatre world. The play is a fairy tale where Griffiths imagines a world in which theatres are run by warring clans, writing, "These are stories of Trish, an underground actress and clan member of ever-beleaguered, Dirty Theatre. At the time this story begins, the theatre is fighting the gathering darkness as Trish is struggling with the forces of clan loyalty" (qtd. in Althof et al. 202). The connection to Starhawk's ecstatic "spiral dance" is made more explicit in a version of the play excerpted in *Taking the Stage*; here Griffiths writes that "[a]t times throughout her story, especially when the story centres on her mysterious illness, [Trish] moves her body in a spiral motion, as if trying to unwind her body from within" (34). Through Trish as her alter ego, Griffiths is clearly seeking ways to integrate her foundational experiences in the theatre world with her feminist belief system, with a way to feel connected with a clan and to make sense of her own life decisions and spiritual quest. As we have seen, Griffiths returns to the idea of loyalty to one's clan through her character Zach. He feels connected to other gamers across the world, and his clan identity is a way to reject the corporate world of his father, much as Trish rejects the corporate world of arts councils

---

8   Starhawk develops these ideas in her books *The Spiral Dance: A Rebirth of the Ancient Religion of the Great Goddess* (1979) and *Dreaming the Dark: Magic, Sex, and Politics* (1982).

and funding grants to pledge her allegiance to artists. But unlike Trish and her theatre clan, Zach cannot live in his alternative world of fantasy games, largely because he is a teenager and must accommodate the adult concerns of his parents, in particular his mother, Marion.

Griffiths uses Marion as a stand-in for herself to explore her relationship to youth culture: sympathetic, eager to understand and relate, but ultimately an outsider. While Griffiths is fascinated with young people, her character Marion is dealing with her own child, and the stakes are therefore heightened. *Games: Who Wants to Play?* is the first time that Griffiths has written a central female character interacting with her child as an important presence on stage. Children have been present in her plays before, but in far more oblique ways. For example, in the course of *Maggie and Pierre*, Maggie goes from being a (flower) child herself to the mother of three, but her children never physically appear on stage and they are repeatedly framed in a negative way. Most seriously, the children are weapons used against her by her husband and by the public, who condemn Maggie by demanding, "What kind of mother could leave those beautiful children?" (88). In an important monologue in which she responds to her critics, Maggie confesses that she does not know who she is supposed to be—"I don't know if I'm a wife or a mother or a career . . . " (89)—and admits that she cannot live up to the image of perfection expected of her. Maggie's search for her identity as a woman continues with Marion. The actor who played Marion in the ATP production, Kate Newby, explained: "It felt as though the character of Marion was a different person in every scene. In the end, I decided Marion's game was to try on different personae/roles. This notion anchored me and gave me an opening into what women constantly face—our ever changing roles and personalities in our search for identity." This struggle for female self-definition is a recurring theme in Griffiths's plays. For example, Patricia Keeney has suggested that another of Griffiths's central female characters, Wallis Simpson in *The Duchess*, can be understood as Griffiths's version of Hedda Gabler: "both women trapped in a world too small for them, disastrously thwarted in their ambitious, narcissistic all-consuming drive to create themselves" (xi–xii). Continuing the comparison with Ibsen's characters, Marion can perhaps be understood as

Griffiths's Mrs. Alving from *Ghosts*: another mother who ends her play in a struggle to save her doomed son.

Marion certainly presents herself as a concerned mother to Zach, worried about the environment, fretting over daily news stories about male adolescent cruelty, terrified by the death of Zach's friend Michael Ferguson. She is supportive of her husband and claims not to be bothered by his impotence (6). But as the play progresses, Marion is seduced by the games that Zach and Micky play, and she convinces them to let her join in. She is exhilarated but physically overwhelmed and vomits into a backpack (26). As her physicality and sexuality are awakened, she responds to Micky's aggressive flirting and kisses him passionately on the stairs that represent the liminal world between adulthood and adolescence (67). In the play's most complex scene for Marion, she tries to involve the three male characters in her own world by dressing up in a new outfit she has bought and modelling it for their feedback and approval. Dan and Micky compliment her, but Zach finds the dress too sexual and revealing and calls her a "ho," provoking a physical confrontation with his father. In Zach's eyes, her sexuality is incompatible with her role as a mother, while Marion is trying desperately to integrate the two. Marion's line to Zach—"I can't see you; your face is distorted. I look to see your sweet face but you've gone. I'm disappearing too" (62)—is extremely telling. While she can see herself as the young mother of a sweet baby boy, she cannot find her identity as the more mature mother of a troubled and withdrawn teenager.

In an important scene with Zach, as they do laundry together, Marion recalls: "I still wasn't sure, even after you began to kick, even after all that agony that's supposed to bond you. I just didn't see myself going all mothery. They put you in my arms and I still didn't feel it. Then you leaned back and looked right into my eyes, as if to say, 'Who have I got as a mother?' And I was yours. I chose you" (45). Again, we see that Marion was able to reconcile herself to mothering a baby, but that she is struggling with how to be herself as a woman with a fifteen-year-old son. Ultimately, she decides to let go of her preoccupation with Zach; instead, she chooses to recommit to Dan and they are able to have sex again (76). As a couple, they consider adopting another son and trying again (70); they agree to cut off Zach's gaming privileges, and they congratulate themselves on finally being good parents and partners. But of course the final scene, in which they offer Zach cuddles while the audience knows the violence he has committed, reveals how deluded they really are. Marion and Dan have had their parenting predetermined by their own cultural scripts and their own needs—for a sweet boy or for a buddy—and they find themselves unable to respond to the son they actually have.

Like her characters Marion and Dan, Linda Griffiths faced the perceived enigma of a younger generation as she developed *Games: Who Wants to Play?* Unlike her characters, however, she found a path that allowed her to respond effectively to the voices and experiences of younger people. After her own experiences with her teenage brother and the children of her friends, Griffiths turned to other sources to make sense of youth gaming culture. Her time with students at the University of Lethbridge, her research into real-life cases like the one that led to the character of Michael Ferguson, and her long developmental process across multiple versions of the play ultimately led her to a portrait of parental failure. Contemporary forces have distorted Zach's passage into young adulthood, and his parents have not been able to offer him an alternative. Griffiths has created a conflicted female adult character to embody her own complex relationship to motherhood and generational divide, and a teenage boy character to embody her fascination with fantasy and alternative cultures. One of Griffiths's final plays, *Games: Who Wants to Play?* stands as a compassionate exploration of themes that preoccupied her throughout her career.

LINDA DID NOT WANT TO BE A BOY, BUT SHE WANTED THEIR STAGE TIME

LAYNE COLEMAN

Below is a diary entry that Linda Griffiths wrote while she was struggling to understand what was happening to her. For me it illuminates her relationship to creativity, turning lemons into lemonade. For Linda, everything had to become art, or a play. Her writing was a search to perform what was going on inside her. To bring meaning to her life: to make the darkness abate and find the humour in all of the attendant folly and seriousness of life.

There was never a more beautiful summer to get cancer. Everywhere a sense of bounty. The summer poured itself around me, a sheath of yellow silk spinning through the streets, the stores and houses, enveloping, merging me with Dr. Gwen, the naturopath. When I went to her about the first diagnoses, she was magnificent. "You have a voice in all this." It felt like being born. I "had a voice" in all this, talking about alternatives to chemotherapy, letting me know the options. As she coached me, she opened her arms and lifted up her hands, "there is energy here," encompassing all of summer, all fruits, vegetables, legumes and grasses, the earth is blooming, that's energy too, that's healing too.

As it was happening this blog voice started to appear, I've hardly ever read a blog but the voice is everywhere—how many cancer bloggers—hundreds of thousands? Just like me, lots of people say they're relieved or released or something when they get the diagnosis, I knew it had to end, I knew I couldn't go on like I was.

Of course I wanted to get something creative out of the cancer, use it girl, or something like that. There's a market out there, god knows, it seems like half the world has cancer and the other half is afraid to get it. How many Oncologists does it take to screw in a lightbulb? Onc Onc.

There was never a more beautiful summer to get cancer.

—Linda Griffiths, Spring 2013

****

FAST FORWARD TO THE LOWER MAINLAND—SURREY

Linda has a gift for naming things. Some of her most important titles that brought a popular explosion at the box office were: *Paper Wheat*; *If You're So Good, Why Are You In Saskatoon?*; *O.D. On Paradise*; *Alien Creature*; *The Last Dog of War*; *The Age of Arousal*; *The Darling Family*; *Heaven Above, Heaven Below*. She was box office gold in Saskatchewan and with *Maggie and Pierre* she cemented it across Canada. The winner of twelve major awards for playwright and actress, she knows the long walk to the podium.

Linda has cancer and I know where this is going. She does too, but she doesn't want to talk about it, so we won't. She says as an illustration, "Think of me as a fat person, I can say I'm fat, but you can't." Fair enough. We go for a walk instead. We are both people of a certain age.

—Layne Coleman, Fall 2013

****

Hi Linda,

I have been asked to write an essay for an anthology of your work. A kind theatre academic wants me to not only create the energy and presence of your personality, but to tell a story. I believe that is the idea. You and I have so many stories together and we could tell it a myriad of ways. "What was it like to work with you?" That is the question I aim to answer. One of our greatest projects together was the Art Farm where we joined ourselves together in a kind of art family. You and I and my daughter Charlotte and whomever Charlotte was dating at the time. We had a good run. You called it an unorthodox family. Those were the happiest years of your life, you said (and probably mine too), but your incoming cancer was there, and makes it hard to express the joy of that time, the mingling of sorrow and joy. When was there not such a time?

Often your titles were the first important step in drawing a crowd. But you knew what to do with them after that, your voice was quick to grow an audience anywhere. I have never met any artist of the theatre who peeked through the curtain before the show like you did, and if there were any empty chairs, it made you furious, like some great opportunity had been lost. No one loved performing as much as you. But you would have made an effective publicist; you had an instinct for framing.

I will focus on Saskatchewan, for you loved it there, and it was where you first discovered your true voice. And the Prairie people embraced you: after your death, Gerry Stoll wrote me a letter that he wanted read at your memorial. Alas, I received the letter too late, but will include it here. Gerry was your favourite impresario and theatre general manager. It's not hard to see why. You met him as the GM of 25th Street Theatre in Saskatoon, a company that you put on the map. Too bad it is gone now.

Gerry Stoll:

In 1977, the entire theatre company was almost broke with just enough money to create one more play. I distinctly recall thinking "this is our last chance" as Layne and I watched Linda plus our little troop of actors set off in a van. The company was to do research/ interviews with pioneers and collectively create a worthy story. They spent several weeks travelling the country roads taking in the history and culture of farm life. Deadlines loomed and it came time to name this play and when the actors were asked for a title these words came from Linda, "Our first farm settlers had it tough (not just the weather and isolation) but also they were under the thumb of the Grain Exchange, where speculators (not farmers) traded futures like paper wheat." For a moment the rehearsal hall went silent . . . *Paper Wheat*. And so Saskatchewan's most successful play (over 50,000 attendance) was named by Linda. Soon the play began touring to farm communities with 100% sell-out houses; standing/cheering ovations every night. The production took on a life of its own. Linda effected a change in Canadian culture . . .

. . . In 1980, *Maggie and Pierre* toured Canada, playing the SUB Theatre (Horowitz Theatre) in Edmonton. Linda filled our 700 seat theatre for every show and went into hold overs. 5,000 people attended, these were rock star numbers! Linda impacted Edmonton's view of Canada.

For me, Linda's greatest triumph is a monologue in 1977's *Paper Wheat*. She portrays an Irish farmer Sean, who is trying to coax his two oxen to plow the sod in a scene. "Breaking the Prairie." Linda used a prop (4 pieces of wood replicating the plow) and transported the audience back into that field. This always received big laughs, many tears and huge applause. When my parents, who were life-long farmers, attended one night (their first play) and were introduced to Linda, my dad said to her, "It was just like that." In four minutes on stage, she had connected the farmer and the actor . . .

****

You did not want to be a boy, but you certainly wanted their stage time.

After you created *Maggie and Pierre*, which was first done in workshop in the Backspace of Theatre Passe Muraille—your collaborative life with Paul Thompson was rolling by this time—everything changed. You became famous, touring that show to all the big theatres in Canada and to New York. You were swimming in celebrity, good notices, and money. The aftermath of that time gave you a bad back and many other illnesses you fought for the rest of your life. In your later life your relationship to your fame was something you turned into a stand-up piece you would perform at parties. You had found what many of us wanted, but because you had achieved your goals early in your life, you were able to become a real writer after that. You drilled down. You focused on the art, on deepening your work and finding the truth in complexity. You worked constantly through hard times refining your plays and finding ways of getting them out to their public.

Aside from being a Canadian nationalist, an Anglophile of television dramas, an avid reader, a listener to CBC Radio, a mentor of young women writers, and the host of artistic salons at your house over a lifetime, you were also a pagan and you were the first to tell me how the Roman Church and Christianity murdered the culture of women, destroying along with that a priceless library of knowledge, all the good that the witches were able to do with all the technology they carried forced underground, criminalized. You carried their secrets in everything you wrote and lived. Your mother and her five sisters from Nova Scotia were raised by their father, a one-armed policeman. All these feminine energies and genes driving you forward. You witnessed your mother's life and suffering, a woman who immigrated to Montreal to find a career and found a husband instead; your father an RAF fighter, twenty-nine missions, many to Berlin, a survivor, a British working-class man who brought his Yorkshire values to Montreal, and there found your mother, that relationship, that living in the first Canadian suburb, Pierrefonds, an English suburb on the outskirts of French Montreal. You experienced sub-urban life abrasively, but you were near forests and fields where you played, alone, and forged relationships to fairies and trees. That life forged a unique artist that gave Canada an understanding of itself, and the life of women. One of your most personal and beautiful one-woman shows was *The Last Dog of War*, about your coming to terms with your father and his life. In that show you took us into the heart of war, a brave and understanding woman in a chair showing us what it was to be a vulnerable boy forced to play a small but incredibly dangerous part in history. You saw movements and characters and culture in mythological frames. You made farmers sexy with *Paper Wheat* and you wrote plays that are being done around the world, telling stories that give women centre stage.

Love,
Layne Coleman

WORKS CITED

Adachi, Ken. "Findley Novel a Sell-Out in London." *Toronto Star*, 6 Apr. 1987, p. B1.

Althof, Rolf, Rurik von Antropff, Klaus Peter Muller, editors. *Inter-plays: Works and Words of Writers and Critics: A Festschrift Published in Honour of Albert-Reiner Glaap*. Breakwater, 1994.

Alvarez, Natalie. "Realisms of Redress: Alameda Theatre and the Formation of a Latina/o-Canadian Theatre and Politics." *New Canadian Realisms*, edited by Roberta Barker and Kim Solga, Playwrights Canada, 2012, pp. 144–62.

Andrews, Jennifer. "Framing *The Book of Jessica*: Transformation and the Collaborative Process in Canadian Theatre." *English Studies in Canada*, vol. 22, no. 3, 1996. pp. 297–313.

Atwood, Margaret. *The Journals of Susanna Moodie*. Oxford UP, 1970.

Barr, Erica. Personal interview with Shelley Scott, 24 Aug. 2016.

Barrie, J.M. *Peter Pan*. 1904. *Peter Pan and Other Plays*, edited by Peter Hollindale, Oxford UP, 1995, pp. 73–154.

Beattie, Steven W. "Playwright and Actor Linda Griffiths Dies at 60." *Quill and Quire*, 22 Sep. 2014, https://quillandquire.com/authors/2014/09/22/playwright-and -actor-linda-griffiths-dies-at-60/.

Bessai, Diane. *Playwrights of Collective Creation*. Simon and Pierre, 1992.

Bloch, Michael. *Operation Willi: The Nazi Plot to Kidnap the Duke of Windsor, July 1940*. Weidenfeld and Nicolson, 1984.

---. *Ribbentrop*. Crown, 1992.

Boardman, Kathleen A. "Autobiography as Collaboration: *The Book of Jessica*." *Textual Studies in Canada/Études textuelles au Canada*, no. 4, 1994, pp. 28–39.

Braem, Meg. Telephone interview with Shelley Scott, 2 Sep. 2016.

Brooks, Daniel, and Daniel MacIvor. "The 14 Plays That Changed Everything for Canadian Theatre." *The Book of Lists*, by Ira Basen and Jane Farrow, Alfred A. Knopf, 2017. *CBC.ca*, 6 Jun. 2017, http://www.cbc.ca/arts/the-14-plays -that-changed-everything-for-canadian-theatre-1.4385954.

Campbell, Maria. *Halfbreed*. Good Read Biographies, 1983.

Carter, Jill. "Decolonizing the *Gathering Place: Chocolate Woman* Dreams a *Gathering House* in Toronto." *Theatre and Performance in Toronto*, edited by Laura Levin, Playwrights Canada, 2011, pp. 176–90. Critical Perspectives on Canadian Theatre in English 21.

Chamberlain, Adrian. "Director Chose Griffiths Play for Abundance of Good Female Roles." *Times-Colonist* [Victoria, BC], 16 Feb. 2017, http://www.timescolonist.com /director-chose-linda-griffiths-play-for-abundance-of-female-roles-1.9970903.

Chester, Blanca, and Valerie Dudoward. "Journeys and Transformations." *Textual Studies in Canada/Études textuelles au Canada*, no. 1, 1991, pp. 156–77.

Clark, Bob. "Griffiths Arouses Greatness: Comic Drama Witty, Inventive." *Calgary Herald*, 17 Feb. 2007. *Proquest*, https://search-proquest-com.ezproxy.lib.ucalgary.ca /docview/245489517/fulltext/99C73521D514CADPQ/1?accountid=9838.

Crew, Robert. "The Spirits are with Tantoo Cardinal." *The Toronto Star*, 16 Nov. 1986, p. E1.

Crook, Barbara. "Three Busy Actresses Meet in One Play; After Years of Roles as Token Indians, Natives Finding Realistic Work." *The Ottawa Citizen*, 21 Oct. 1986, p. D17.

Debenham, Diane. "Native People in Contemporary Canadian Drama." *Canadian Drama*, no. 14, 1998, pp. 137–58.

Dolan, Jill. *Utopia in Performance: Finding Hope at the Theater*. U of Michigan P, 2005. *ProQuest Ebook Central*, https://ebookcentral-proquest-com.ezproxy.lib.ucalgary.ca /lib/ucalgary-ebooks/detail.action?docID=3414662.

Donnelly, Pat. "Linda Griffiths was 'A Lovely, Kind and Fiercely Authentic Artist.'" *Montreal Gazette*, 22 Sep. 2014, http://www.montrealgazette.com/entertainment /Linda+Griffiths+lovely+kind+fiercely+authentic+artist/10225564/story.html.

Donovan, Kevin, and Jesse Brown. "CBC Fires Jian Ghomeshi over Sex Allegations." *Toronto Star*, 26 Oct. 2014, https://www.thestar.com/news/canada/2014/10/26/cbc_fires_jian _ghomeshi_over_sex_allegations.html.

Egan, Susanna. "*The Book of Jessica*: The Healing Circle of a Woman's Autobiography." *Canadian Literature*, no. 144, 1995, pp. 10–26.

Faludi, Susan. *Backlash: The Undeclared War Against American Women*. Anchor Books, 1991.

Field, Tom. *Secrets in the Shadows: The Art & Life of Gene Colan*. TwoMorrows, 2005.

Findley, Timothy. *Famous Last Words*. Penguin, 1982.

---. "The King and Mrs. Simpson." *Toronto Life*, May 1984, pp. 32–33.

Ford, Garret. "Social and Emotional Aspects of World of Warcraft Players." Master of Education thesis, University of Lethbridge, 2016.

Forsyth, Jessie. "'A Combination of the Spontaneous and the Strained': Collision, Transformation and *The Book of Jessica*." *The Canadian Journal of Native Studies*, vol. 36, no. 1, 2016, pp. 57–79.

Gill, Rosalind. "Post-postfeminism?: New Feminist Visibilities in Postfeminist Times." *Feminist Media Studies*, vol. 16, no. 4, 2016, pp. 610–30. *Taylor & Francis Online*, http://www-tandfonline-com.ezproxy.lib.ucalgary.ca/doi/abs/10.1080/14680777.2016.1193293.

Gilmore, Leigh. *Autobiographics: A Feminist Theory of Women's Self-Representation*. Cornell UP, 1994.

Gissing, George. *The Odd Women*. 1893. Edited by Patricia Ingham, Oxford UP, 2000.

Gladstone, Amiel. Email correspondence with Shelley Scott, 21 Oct. and 24 Oct. 2016.

Goldman, Jessica. "Games: Who Wants to Play?" *Applause! Meter*, 16 Mar. 2014, https://applause-meter.com/2014/03/16/games-review/.

Griffiths, Linda. *Age of Arousal*. Coach House, 2007.

---. *Alien Creature: a visitation from Gwendolyn MacEwen*. Playwrights Canada, 2000.

---. *Chronic*. Playwrights Canada, 2004.

---. *The Darling Family: A Duet for Three*. Blizzard, 1991.

---. *The Duchess: AKA Wallis Simpson. Maggie and Pierre & The Duchess*. Playwrights Canada, 2013, pp. 103–230.

---. "A Flagrantly Weird Age: A Reaction to Research, Time Travel and the History of the Suffragettes." *Age of Arousal*, by Griffiths, Coach House, 2007, pp. 135–68.

---. "Further Reading." *Age of Arousal*, by Griffiths, Coach House, 2007, pp. 169–72.

---. *A Game of Inches. Sheer Nerve*, by Griffiths, Blizzard, 1999, pp. 181–237.

---. *Games to be Played with Caution*. Draft #6, 27 Sep. 2010. Unpublished manuscript.

---. *Games: Who Wants to Play?* Playwrights Canada, 2016.

---. "I Am a Thief . . . Not Necessarily Honourable Either." *Theatre and AutoBiography: Writing and Performing Lives in Theory and Practice*, edited by Sherrill Grace and Jerry Wasserman, Talon, 2006, pp. 301–05.

---. "Interview." *Canadian Theatre Review*, vol. 97, winter 1998, pp. 57–61.

---. *The Last Dog of War*. Playwrights Canada, 2016.

---. *The Last Dog of War*. 4 Jul. 2005, Archival & Special Collections, McLaughlin Library, University of Guelph. Transcript.

---. *The Last Dog of War*. Apr. 2007, Archival & Special Collections, McLaughlin Library, University of Guelph. Unpublished manuscript.

---. *The Last Dog of War*. 4 Feb. 2009, Archival & Special Collections, McLaughlin Library, University of Guelph. Unpublished manuscript.

---. *The Last Dog of War*. 10 Oct. 2011, Archival & Special Collections, McLaughlin Library, University of Guelph. Unpublished manuscript.

---. "*The Last Dog of War*: A History of the Process of Development." *Linda Griffiths*, http://www.lindagriffiths.ca/media/pdfs/Process_The_Last_Dog_of_War.pdf.

---. "Last dog order." No date, Archival & Special Collections, McLaughlin Library, University of Guelph.

---. *Maggie and Pierre*. *Maggie and Pierre & The Duchess*, by Griffiths, Playwrights Canada, 2013, pp. 29–92.

---. *O.D. on Paradise*. *Sheer Nerve*, by Griffiths, Blizzard, 1999, pp. 35–93.

---. Personal interview with Shelley Scott, 20 Sep. 2011.

---. "Playwright's Note." *Age of Arousal*, by Griffiths, Coach House, 2007, pp. 8–22.

---. "Playwright's Note: *Age of Arousal*." Program, Enbridge playRites Festival of New Canadian Plays, Alberta Theatre Projects, EPCOR Centre for the Performing Arts, Calgary, 31 Jan.–4 Mar. 2007, p. 8.

---. "Playwright's Note: *Games: Who Wants to Play?*" Program, Enbridge playRites Festival of New Canadian Plays, Alberta Theatre Projects, EPCOR Centre for the Performing Arts, Calgary, 7 Mar.–5 Apr. 2014, pp. 10–11.

---. "Process?" *Canadian Theatre Review*, vol. 97, winter 1998, pp. 57–61.

---. Public talk. David Spinks Theatre, University of Lethbridge, 23 Sep. 2011.

---. *Sheer Nerve: Seven Plays*. Blizzard, 1999.

---. *Spiral Woman & The Dirty Theatre. Taking the Stage: Selections from Plays by Canadian Women*, edited by Cynthia Zimmerman, Playwrights Canada, 1994, pp. 34–38.

---. "Subject: 49 squadron." Received by D.C. Boughton, 6 Nov. 2004. Archival & Special Collections, McLaughlin Library, University of Guelph.

Griffiths, Linda, and Maria Campbell. *The Book of Jessica: A Theatrical Transformation*. Coach House, 1989.

Griffiths, Linda, and Kathleen Gallagher. "Improvisation and Risk: A Dialogue with Linda Griffiths." *How Theatre Educates: Conversations and Counterpoints with Artists, Scholars, and Advocates*, edited by Gallagher and David Booth, U of Toronto P, 2003, pp. 114–30.

Guist, Sean. Email correspondence with Shelley Scott, 2 Oct. 2016.

Hanrahan, Gail. Personal interview with Shelley Scott, 24 Aug. 2016.

Highway, Tomson. *The Rez Sisters*. Fifth House, 1988.

Hines, Karen. Telephone interview with Shelley Scott, 25 Oct. 2016.

Hnath, Lucas. *A Doll's House, Part 2*. Theatre Communications Group, 2018.

Hobson, Louis. "Games: Who Wants to Play a Topnotch Drama." *Calgary Sun*, 17 Mar. 2014, http://www.calgarysun.com/2014/03/17/games-who-wants-to-play-a-topnotch-drama.

Hoy, Helen. "'When You Admit You're A Thief, Then You Can Be Honourable': Native / Non-Native Collaboration in *The Book of Jessica*." *Canadian Literature*, no. 136, 1993, pp 24–39.

Hutcheon, Linda, with Siobhan Flynn. *A Theory of Adaptation*. 2nd ed., Routledge, 2013. *ProQuest Ebook Central*, https://ebookcentral-proquest-com.ezproxy.lib.ucalgary.ca/lib/ucalgary-ebooks/detail.action?docID=1016075.

Hyatt, Lauren. Email correspondence with Shelley Scott, 29 Aug. 2016.

Ibsen, Henrik. *A Doll's House*. 1879. *Four Major Plays*, by Ibsen, translated by James McFarlane and Jens Arup, Oxford UP, 2008, pp. 1–86.

Ingham, Patricia. Introduction. *The Odd Women*, by George Gissing, edited by Ingham, Oxford UP, 2000, pp. vii–xxv.

Jacklin, Michael. "Collaboration, Circulation, and the Question of Counterfeit in *The Book of Jessica*." *Dalhousie Review*, vol. 93, no. 1, 2013, p. 121–39.

Jefferess, David. "Whose Story is it, Anyway? Or, Power and Difference in *The Book of Jessica*: Implications for Theories of Collaboration." *English Studies in Canada*, vol. 29, nos. 3 and 4, Sep.–Dec. 2003, pp. 220–41.

Johnson, Brian D. "Masks of a Métis Star." *Maclean's*, 20 Oct. 1986, p. 63–64.

Keeney, Patricia. "Mythologizing the Wilderness: An Introduction to Linda Griffiths." *Maggie and Pierre & The Duchess*, Playwrights Canada, 2013, pp. iii–xii.

Keeshig-Tobias, Lenore. "Stop Stealing Native Stories." *Borrowed Power: Essays on Cultural Appropriation*, edited by Bruce Ziff and Pratima V. Rao, Rutgers UP, 1997, pp. 71–73.

Kelly, Katherine E. "Making the Bones Sing: The Feminist History Play, 1976–2010." *Contemporary Women Playwrights: Into the Twenty-First Century*, edited by Penny Farfan and Lesley Ferris, Palgrave Macmillan, 2013, pp. 199–214.

Knowles, Ric. General Editor's Preface. *Performing Indigeneity*, edited by Yvette Nolan and Knowles, Playwrights Canada, 2016, pp. v–vii. New Essays on Canadian Theatre 6.

Lauzon, Jani, and Beatriz Pizano. Talkback session on *Alien Creature*. 26 Jan. 2017, Theatre Passe Muraille, Toronto.

Lawson, Robert. "The Nazi Who Loved Canada." *Globe and Mail*, 9 Sep. 2006, p. F3.

Lane, Richard J. "Sacred Community, Sacred Culture: Authenticity and Modernity in Contemporary Canadian Native Writings." *Native Authenticity: Transnational Perspectives on Native American Literary Studies*, edited by Deborah L. Madsen, Suny, 2010, pp. 151–65.

Leeper, Muriel. "Linda Griffiths: The Actress as Playwright." *Canadian Theatre Review*, vol. 38, fall 1983, pp.110–13.

Levin, Laura. Introduction. *Theatre and Performance in Toronto*, edited by Levin, Playwrights Canada, 2011, pp. vii–xvi.

"Linda Griffiths on Creation, Purpose and Meaning (Part 5 of 17)." *Theatre Museum Canada: The Legend Library*, interview by Andrew Moodie, Theatre Museum Canada, 23 Jan. 2013. *YouTube*, 1 Nov. 2017, https://www.youtube.com/watch?v=JPqZZLPBqS4&list=PLgHeSy6OB4x6nzjnxVAANivRbIXX1H-xS&index=4.

"Linda Griffiths on Saskatoon, Collective Creation and Paul Thompson (Part 4 of 17)." *Theatre Museum Canada: The Legend Library*, interview by Andrew Moodie, Theatre Museum Canada, 23 Jan. 2013. *YouTube*, 1 Nov. 2017, https://www.youtube.com/watch?v=vQlIjP_ueNA&index=3&list=PLgHeSy6OB4x6nzjnxVAANivRbIXX1H-xS.

"LINDA GRIFFITHS ~ Talks About Her 5 Solo Shows at SOULO Festival 2014." *YouTube*, uploaded by Tracey Erin Smith, 27 Sep. 2014, https://www.youtube.com/watch?v=lJ358nkSFWo.

Lomon, Cameron. Personal interview with Shelley Scott, 24 Aug. 2016.

MacEwen, Gwendolyn. *Afterworlds*. McClelland and Stewart, 1987.

---. *A Breakfast for Barbarians*. Ryerson UP, 1966.

---. *The Fire-Eaters*. Oberon, 1976.

---. *Gwendolyn MacEwen, Volume One: The Early Years*. Exile, 1993.

---. *Gwendolyn MacEwen, Volume Two: The Later Years*. Exile, 1994.

---. *King of Egypt, King of Dreams*. Macmillan, 1971.

---. *The Rising Fire*. Contact, 1963.

---. *The Shadow-Maker*. Macmillan, 1969.

---. *The T.E. Lawrence Poems*. Mosaic, 1982.

Makahonuk, Glen. *25th Street Theatre Collection: A Finding Aid*. 1988. *University of Saskatchewan Library*, https://primo-pmtna02.hosted.exlibrisgroup.com /primo-explore/fulldisplay?docid=USaskIII.b33162293&context=L&vid =USASK&search_scope=UofS&tab=default_tab&lang=en_US.

Maltby, Clive, director. *Britain's Nazi King?* Oxford Film and Television, 2009.

Maracle, Lee. "Moving Over." *Trivia*, no. 14, spring 1989, pp. 9–12.

Martin, Ralph. *The Woman He Loved*. Simon and Schuster, 1974.

McLeod, Katherine. "(Un)Covering the Mirror: Performative Reflections in Linda Griffiths's *Alien Creature: A Visitation from Gwendolyn MacEwen* and Wendy Lill's *The Occupation of Heather Rose*." *Solo Performance*, edited by Jenn Stephenson, Playwrights Canada, 2010, pp. 141–54. Critical Perspectives on Canadian Theatre in English 20.

---. "(Un)Covering the Mirror: Performative Reflections in Linda Griffiths's *Alien Creature: A Visitation from Gwendolyn MacEwen* and Wendy Lill's *The Occupation of Heather Rose*." *Theatre and Autobiography: Writing and Performing Lives in Theory and Practice*, edited by Sherill Grace and Jerry Wasserman, Talon, 2006, pp. 89–104.

McRobbie, Angela. "Post-Feminism and Popular Culture." *Feminist Media Studies*, vol. 4, no. 3, 2004, pp. 255–64. *Taylor & Francis Online*, http://www-tandfonline-com .ezproxy.lib.ucalgary.ca/doi/abs/10.1080/1468077042000309937.

Mietkiewicz, Henry. "Daring to be Different is a Darling Quality in Film Playwright/ Actress Linda Griffiths Dares to Take a Chance on 'What Matters to Me.'" *Toronto Star*, 28 Aug. 1994, p. B3.

Morton, Andrew. *17 Carnations: The Royals, the Nazis, and the Biggest Cover-Up in History*. Grand Central, 2015.

Murray, Laura J. "Economies of Experience in *The Book of Jessica*." *Tulsa Studies in Women's Literature*, vol. 18, no. 1, 1999, pp. 91–111.

Myles, Ruth. "Games Comes Out a Draw at playRites." *Calgary Herald*, 18 Mar. 2014, https://calgaryherald.com/entertainment/ruth-myles-games-comes-out-a-draw-at-playrites.

Nestruck, Kelly J. "Playwright and Actor Linda Griffiths Dies from Cancer." *Globe and Mail*, 21 Sep. 2014, https://www.theglobeandmail.com/arts/theatre-and-performance /playwright-and-actor-linda-griffiths-dies-from-cancer/article20713788/.

Newby, Kate. Email correspondence with Shelley Scott, 29 Oct. 2016.

Perrault, Jeanne. "Writing Whiteness: Raced Subjectivity in *The Book of Jessica*." *Essays on Canadian Writing*, winter 1996, pp. 14–31.

Petrasek, Michael. "Research on the Work of Linda Griffiths." Received by Amanda Attrell, 12 Jan. 2016.

Phelan, Peggy. *Unmarked: The Politics of Performance*. Routledge, 1993.

Phillips, Adrian. *The King Who Had to Go: Edward VIII, Mrs. Simpson, and the Hidden Politics of the Abdication Crisis*. Biteback, 2016.

"Playwright Linda Griffiths." *Theatre Museum Canada: The Legend Library*, interview by Andrew Moodie, Theatre Museum Canada, 23 Jan. 2013. *YouTube*, 1 Nov. 2017, https://www.youtube.com/playlist?list=PLgHeSy6OB4x6nzjnxVAANivRbIXX1H-xS.

Pound, Ezra. "H. S. Mauberley (Life and Contexts)." *Selected Poems*, edited with an introduction by T.S. Eliot, Faber, 1948, pp. 117–38.

Preston, Jennifer. "Weesageechak Begins to Dance: Native Earth Performing Arts Inc." *The Drama Review*, vol. 36, no. 1, spring 1992, pp. 135–59.

Prokosh, Kevin. "Play Wins Arousing Round of Applause." *Winnipeg Free Press*, 21 Mar. 2009, https://www.winnipegfreepress.com/arts-and-life/entertainment/arts /play-wins-arousing-round-of-applause-41620357.html.

Rodgers, Sarah. "Behind the Bewitching Force of Wallis Simpson: The King's Mrs." *Maggie and Pierre & The Duchess*, by Linda Griffiths, Playwrights Canada, 2013, pp. 97–100.

Rudakoff, Judith. "Playwright Linda Griffiths." *Fair Play: 12 Women Speak: Conversations with Canadian Playwrights*. Edited by Rudakoff and Rita Much, Simon & Pierre, 1990, pp. 13–36.

Sanders, Julie. *Adaptation and Appropriation*. Routledge, 2006.

Saul, Joanne. "What Nation? Whose Story? History, Myth, and Collaboration in the Making of *Jessica*." *Essays in Theatre/Études théatrales*, vol. 19, no. 2, May 2001, pp. 141–54.

Scobie, Stephen. "Eye-Deep in Hell: Ezra Pound, Timothy Findley, and Hugh Selwyn Mauberley." *Essays in Canadian Writing*, vol. 30, 1984–1985, pp. 206–27.

Scott, Shelley. "Bodies, Form and Nature: Three Canadian Plays and Reproductive Choice in the 1990s." *British Journal of Canadian Studies*, vol. 17, no. 2, 2004, pp. 197–209.

---. "Sickness and Sexuality: Feminism and the Female Body in *Age of Arousal* and *Chronic*." *Theatre Research in Canada*, vol. 31, no. 1, 2010, pp. 37–56. *Academic One File*, http://link.galegroup.com.ezproxy.lib.ucalgary.ca/apps/doc/A285088459/AONE?u=ucalgary&sid=AONE&xid=ca13bc22.

Sebba, Anne. *That Woman: The Life of Wallis Simpson*. St. Martin's, 2016.

Showalter, Elaine. *Sexual Anarchy: Gender and Culture at the Fin de Siècle*. Viking, 1990.

Starhawk. *Dreaming the Dark: Magic, Sex, and Politics*. Beacon, 1982.

---. *The Spiral Dance: A Rebirth of the Ancient Religion of the Great Goddess*. Harper and Row, 1979.

Stasiulis, Daiva. "'Authentic Voice': Anti-Racist Politics in Canadian Feminist Publishing and Literary Production." *Feminism and the Politics of Difference*, edited by Sneja Gunew and Anna Yeatman, Fernwood, 1993, pp. 35–60.

Stephenson, Jenn. "Introduction: Solo Performance." *Solo Performance*. Playwrights Canada, 2011. Critical Perspectives on Canadian Theatre in English 20.

---. *Performing Autobiography: Contemporary Canadian Drama*. U of Toronto P, 2013.

Stroich, Vicki. Telephone interview with Shelley Scott, 14 Oct. 2016.

Sullivan, Rosemary. *Shadow Maker: The Life of Gwendolyn MacEwen*. HarperCollins, 1995.

Taylor, Bill. "Mojica's Role Her Birthright." *Toronto Star*, 4 Apr. 1986, p. D18.

Tompkins, Joanne. "Infinitely Rehearsing Performance and Identity: *Afrika Solo* and *The Book of Jessica*." *Canadian Theatre Review*, no. 74, spring 1993. pp. 35–39.

Urbach, Karina. *Go-Betweens for Hitler*. Oxford UP, 2015.

Venema, Kathleen. "'Who Reads Plays, Anyway'? The Theory of Drama and The Practice of Rupture in *The Book of Jessica*." *Open Letter*, vol. 9, no. 5, fall 1995, pp. 32–43.

Warner, Andrea. "*The Duchess a.k.a. Wallis Simpson* Makes Sense of a Maligned Woman." *The Georgia Straight*, 1 Apr. 2015.

Wasserman, Jerry. "Alien Creatures and the Ecology of Illness: Linda Griffiths' *Chronic*." Introduction. *Chronic*, by Linda Griffiths, Playwrights Canada, 2004, pp. i–iv.

---. "George Ryga." *Modern Canadian Plays*, edited by Wasserman, vol. 1, 5th ed., Talon, 2012, pp. 23–26.

---. "Linda Griffiths." *Modern Canadian Plays*, edited by Wasserman, vol. 2, 5th ed., Talon, 2013, pp. 387–90.

Weeks, Jeffrey. *Coming Out: Homosexual Politics in Britain from the Nineteenth Century to the Present*. Quartet Books, 1977. *EBSCOhost*, http://web.b.ebscohost.com.ezproxy .lib.ucalgary.ca/ehost/command/detail?vid=0&sid=3e1c5c4d-71c0-4977-b2b3 -e9c00eaa6b8e%40sessionmgr101&bdata=JnNpdGU9ZWhvc3QtbGl2ZQ%3d%3d#jid =8464&db=qth.

Wente, Margaret. "The Lost Boys: Video Games More Fun Than Growing Up." *The Globe and Mail*, 20 Aug. 2016, p. F7.

Wood, Brent. "No-Man's Land: Mythic Crisis in *The T.E. Lawrence Poems*." *Studies in Canadian Literature*, vol. 29, no. 2, summer 2004, pp. 141–62.

York, Lorraine. *Rethinking Women's Collaborative Writing: Power, Difference, Property*. U of Toronto P, 2002.

Zimmerman, Cynthia. "Introducing Wallis." *The Duchess a.k.a. Wallis Simpson*, Playwrights Canada, 1998, pp. i–viii.

ABOUT THE CONTRIBUTORS

Amanda Attrell is a Ph.D. candidate in the Department of English at York University. Her dissertation, entitled *The Theatre of Linda Griffiths*, studies Griffiths's career in relation to the development of Canadian theatre and the work of other women playwrights in Canada.

Layne Coleman is a former artistic director of Theatre Passe Muraille. He was awarded the Rita Davies Award by the Toronto Arts Council for contributions to the arts in Toronto. He was honoured with the George Luscombe Mentorship Award and the Silver Ticket Award by the Toronto Association of Professional Theatres for lifetime achievement in the theatre. He lives in Toronto and has one daughter, Charlotte, who is a writer and is married. He lost his wife, Carole Corbeil—a journalist; theatre, art, and dance critic; as well as a novelist—in the year 2000 to cancer. His short story, "Oasis of Hope," was about that experience and was published in *The Walrus* and was nominated for a National Magazine Award.

Penny Farfan is Professor of Drama at the University of Calgary and the author of *Women, Modernism, and Performance* (Cambridge University Press, 2004) and *Performing Queer Modernism* (Oxford University Press, 2017), as well as many articles and book chapters on modernism and performance and on contemporary women playwrights. She is also the co-editor with Lesley Ferris of *Contemporary Women Playwrights: Into the Twenty-First Century* (Palgrave Macmillan, 2013) and a past editor of *Theatre Journal*.

Sherrill Grace, OC, is Professor Emerita of English and a UBC University Killam Professor. She has published extensively on Canadian literature with books on Margaret Atwood, Malcolm Lowry, the Canadian North, and Tom Thomson. She has co-edited books on Canadian drama and on theatre and autobiography, and she published *Making Theatre: A Life of Sharon Pollock* in 2008. Her biography of Timothy Findley, *Hope Against Despair*, will appear in 2019.

Daniel MacIvor is originally from Cape Breton and currently divides his time between Toronto and Nova Scotia. Daniel has written numerous award-winning theatre productions, including *See Bob Run*, *Never Swim Alone*, *A Beautiful View*, and *His Greatness*. His work has been translated into French, Portuguese, Spanish, Czech, German, and Japanese. With Daniel Brooks he created the solo shows *House*, *Here Lies Henry*, *Monster*, *Cul-de-sac*, *This Is What Happens Next*, and *Who Killed Spalding Gray?* Daniel received the Governor General's Literary Award for Drama for his collection of plays *I Still Love You* and he was awarded the Siminovitch Prize for Theatre. Also a screenwriter, he has written the films *Marion Bridge*, *Wilby Wonderful*, *Trigger*, and *Weirdos*, for which he won a Canadian Screen Award for best original screenplay.

Jacqueline Petropoulos is Adjunct Faculty in English at York University, where she teaches courses in drama studies and Canadian literature. She has published articles in *The Feminist Review*, *Canadian Theatre Review*, *The Malcolm Lowry Review*, and *Signatures of the Past: Cultural Memory in Contemporary Anglophone North American Drama*. She is Assistant Editor of *L.M. Montgomery's Ephraim Weber: Letters 1916–1941*.

Shelley Scott is a professor in the Department of Drama at the University of Lethbridge. She has published two articles dealing with plays by Linda Griffiths: "Sickness and Sexuality: Feminism and the Female Body in *Age of Arousal* and *Chronic*" in *Theatre Research in Canada/Recherches théâtrales au Canada* and "Bodies, Form and Nature: Three Canadian Plays and

Reproductive Choice in the 1990s" in the *British Journal of Canadian Studies*, which includes a discussion of *The Darling Family*. She has also published a review of *Sheer Nerve* and an overview of Griffiths's career in *Theatre Research in Canada/Recherches théâtrales au Canada*.

Paul Thompson was born in Charlottetown, PEI, and grew up in Listowel and Guelph, Ontario. This background later inspired him to create theatre collectively in and about rural Ontario, with such celebrated productions as *The Farm Show, 1837: The Farmers' Revolt*, and *Under the Greywacke*. After a brief stint at the Stratford Festival, Paul joined ranks with Jim Garrard at Theatre Passe Muraille in Toronto, and would later become artistic director of the theatre from 1970 to 1982. Later, Thompson served as director general of the National Theatre School of Canada from 1987 to 1991. He has been appointed an Officer of the Order of Canada, and has received the Governor General's Lifetime Achievement Award for the Performing Arts as well as honorary doctorates from Western University and Algoma University.

Ann Wilson is Director of the School of English and Theatre Studies at the University of Guelph. She is a lead researcher, with Leslie Allin and Dorothy Hadfield, to create online biographies about Canadian women playwrights. This project is one of a number of projects within the Canadian Writing Research Collaboratory. She has written extensively about contemporary Canadian theatre.

Brent Wood teaches in the Department of English and Drama at the University of Toronto at Mississauga. He studies poetry in performance and has published critical works on Gwendolyn MacEwen, Robert Bringhurst, William S. Burroughs, hip-hop rhyming, the Grateful Dead, and many others.

INDEX

Printed on Rolland Enviro, which contains 100% post-consumer
fiber and manufactured using renewable biogas energy.
It is certified FSC®, Processed Chlorine Free,
Ancient Forest Friendly and ECOLOGO 2771.